The
JOHN MILLS
Classical Guitar
TUTOR

£1-0

MUSICAL NEW SERVICES
Distributed by
Music Sales Limited,
8/9 Frith Street, London W1V 5TZ, England.
Music Sales Pty. Limited,
120 Rothschild Avenue, Rosebery NSW 2018, Australia.

© 1981 Musical New Services Limited
© 1989 and 1992 Music Sales Limited
Order No MN 10038
ISBN 0-86175-170-1

Cover design by Ward Peacock Partnership
Book design, typesetting & music processing by Seton Music Graphics
Printed in the United Kingdom by
Caligraving Limited, Thetford, Norfolk.

Music Sales' complete catalogue lists thousands of titles
and is free from your local music shop,
or direct from Music Sales Limited.
Please send a cheque/postal order for £1.50 for postage to:
Music Sales Limited, Newmarket Road, Bury St. Edmunds, Suffolk IP33 3YB.

Preface

It must be the aim of most performers to write a tutor book in which one's own views can be expressed fully, in such a way that many others may benefit from a better understanding of the complexities of learning a musical instrument.

There has never been a substitute for a good teacher; a book may contain a mass of information but it can never identify and correct faults. This means that for the beginner who wishes to go it alone, working from only a book, a highly self-critical approach is essential. To put it in a nutshell, a book can tell you what to do but it can never tell you when you are going wrong.

Most guitar teachers I have spoken to, and this amounts to hundreds in various parts of the world, has his or her different views on teaching, and the actual basics can vary from country to country. In writing this method I have not tried to play safe by steering a middle course. I have my own definite views on teaching and I have used them as a guide in compiling this book.

Each piece has been carefully selected to cover a certain aspect of technique or theory, and provides a smooth progression from one chapter to the next. Just about every period has been referred to, and I am particularly happy to be able to introduce specially composed new pieces towards the end of the book. There are a number of pieces by the established 19th century masters such as Sor, Giuliani, etc. which no tutor would be complete without, but to balance this there are examples from other periods, including works by Dowland, Sanz, Bach, etc.

I have heard it said that there are no secrets in classical guitar playing. This, I think, is true; with this tutor I have tried to explain the process of learning in a simple and straightforward way. Certainly there should be no secrets in playing the guitar, just good taste, judgement, a sincere love of music and lastly, but by no means least, common sense combined with hard work.

This is the second edition of the tutor, and I have updated and amended it substantially, using new pieces where appropriate.

May I wish you every success in your studies.

John Mills
London, England
February 1992

Contents

1. CHOOSING AN INSTRUMENT

Before going on to the complexities of actually playing the classical guitar, we should look first of all at the instrument itself and the various points to check on when purchasing one, whether it be a beginner's model or a concert instrument.

My first tip is spend the most you can afford – it is worth it in the long run. Classical guitars always have nylon strings, and are basically very simple instruments in appearance, with only a little inlay around the soundhole and along the edge of the front, back and sides. Do not be taken in by the eager shop assistant who claims that the brilliantly coloured steel-string guitar advertised as their special model at 25% off if bought this week, will do the job perfectly if fitted with nylon strings. Steel-string guitars are built differently, and do not work properly with other sorts of strings.

The beauty of the classical guitar is in its graceful shape, and the selection of woods. The top, or front of the guitar is usually made of spruce or cedar, and is quite thin, between 2 mm and 3 mm. Underneath this front there is a system of struts which support it, and help to transmit vibrations from the bridge over the whole area of the front, strengthening the sound, and determining the basic tonal character of the instrument. The grain on the front should be straight and even (figure 1). Student instruments usually have cedar fronts, as this timber is more readily available and therefore less expensive than spruce. Cedar is also used, however, on some of the very finest guitars, and produces a strong, warm tone with plenty of volume. Spruce gives a different sound, close to, the guitar can sound softer, but this is deceptive as these instruments very often project exceptionally well in larger halls. The tone tends to be focused, smooth, and has great clarity and balance.

Laminated fronts should be avoided if possible, as the glue joining the layers tends to dry out after a few months, and the guitar's tone and volume suffer quite markedly. Backs and sides can, however, be made from laminated wood, indeed student instruments usually are. However, if you can afford it, go for a guitar with solid back and sides. The timber generally used is rosewood, either Indian (Bombay), or on the better concert guitars Brazilian (Rio) rosewood. The fingerboard should be of ebony, although good quality rosewood is perfectly acceptable. Necks are generally either mahogany or cedar, and there should be no warping at all in the timber. Check by sighting along the edge of the fingerboard looking along the ends of the frets from the nut to the bridge. Another check is to see that the instrument basically plays in tune. This is tested by pressing each string at the twelfth fret, (after the guitar has been tuned to concert pitch, A = 440), and then comparing the stopped note with the open string which should sound exactly an octave lower. This can be a difficult check for a beginner, so if possible try to take a friend who plays to the shop with you. Also make sure the bridge is not lifting away at any point, and that the body of the guitar has no rattles. (Rattles can often be detected by tapping very gently with the knuckles at various points on the front and back of the guitar.) If a rattle is heard, it could be something loose in the machine heads, or possibly the end of a string touching the guitar front at the back of the bridge, both of which are easily corrected. If the rattle persists, this usually means there is something loose inside the guitar, perhaps one of the struts, and this, of course, demands expert attention.

Fig. 1

Check to see that all the joints are secure, particularly at the heel, and that none of the purfling is loose. Each of the frets must be bedded firmly into the fingerboard, and a final check, which is better done at the time of buying the guitar, is the height of the strings above the frets, or "action" as it is called. If the strings are too low, they will buzz on the frets – too high and they will make the guitar extremely difficult to play. Perhaps there will be somebody in the music shop who can test this for you, and if need be have it rectified. Failing this, as soon as possible take the instrument to a friend who already plays, and have them check the action out. If it needs adjustment, go back to the shop where you bought the guitar and tell them what you want to have done. A guitar's action is determined by the performer, and this can differ from player to player but with experience you will become acquainted with this side of playing. However, a badly adjusted action, that is one which is too high, can make learning extremely painful for the left hand, so it is important to get a problem like this sorted out right at the beginning.

In addition to buying the guitar, three other items are essential:
1. A footstool, probably of the folding variety.
2. Something to carry the guitar around in, either a soft waterproof cover, or better still a hard case.
3. A tuning fork pitched at A = 440, (when struck it vibrates at 440 beats per second, so giving you a reliable means of keeping your guitar at correct pitch).

The footstool is made specifically for classical guitarists, and this together with the tuning fork will cost just a few pounds. Soft guitar covers are relatively inexpensive, but unfortunately this is not true of hard cases. It is suggested that for a student model guitar at the cheaper end of the market, a soft cover will do the job – however, for a better class of instrument, a hard case is always advisable.

There is one further item which should be obtained at some time, and that is a folding music stand, although you may find that you can do without one for the first few weeks or months (a lowish table is a pretty good substitute).

To end this opening chapter, a few points about looking after your guitar.

1. When it is not being used, always keep the guitar in its case or cover.
2. Never leave the guitar near a heater as severe damage can be caused.
3. People who have central heating in their houses must take particular care to see that the air does not become too dry, as this can lead to the guitar cracking. Hygrometers are fairly inexpensive, and should be used throughout the winter months. If the air dries out a Dampit should be used in the guitar. (These Dampits can be obtained from most music shops.)
4. Avoid leaving your guitar on a chair or propped against the wall as this is asking for trouble. A table top is one of the safer places, or if it has to stand against a wall, make sure it is in one corner of your bedroom or somewhere quiet where there is no danger of it getting knocked over.

5. Those with hard cases, make sure you hold the lid open when taking out or putting away your guitar, as the front of the instrument is very easily damaged.
6. When picking up the case, always ensure the clasps are secured.
7. Keep machine heads working smoothly by applying a very little light motor grease with the end of a match, working it in by gently turning the gears (lowering the pitch of the strings first before taking them back up to pitch). Any excess grease should be wiped off carefully.
8. Clean the guitar regularly by using a clean soft cloth. The strings should be wiped before and after practising. Do not use any form of polish for brightening up the appearance of the guitar; these polishes, particularly those with a silicone content, are harmful to tone if used over a period of time. If it is absolutely essential to polish the guitar, use a wax polish very sparingly.
9. The timbers of the guitar under normal conditions should need no attention. However, those with central heating may care to apply a light coating of linseed-oil to the finger-board, to protect it against splitting. Probably the best time to do this is during the autumn.
10. Frets do not last for ever, and occasionally it is necessary to have the guitar re-fretted. How long the frets will last depends on the amount of practice you do, but as a rough indication for someone doing about two hours a day, the frets would probably last about 2½ to 3 years before they became hollowed out and needed replacing.

2 HOW TO HOLD THE GUITAR

It cannot be stressed enough how important it is to have a good sitting position when playing the guitar. Any faults in this respect lead to tension problems, which in turn can result in deterioration of performance, and indeed health. (I would brand all guitars with the words "guitar playing can damage your health".) Seriously, a faulty playing position so easily triggers off back problems which can take months, even years to put right.

Firstly, what kind of chair should be used? A simple wooden dining or office type chair without arms is the best. Avoid playing the guitar sitting on soft chairs or couches, as these are very bad for posture. I even had a student once who, when I questioned her about her practice methods, said that she perched herself on the edge of her bed to play!

So a firm solid chair is essential. You will have noticed that the folding type of footstool has several notches, each one giving a different height. I suggest you try one of the middle settings to begin with. Place the footstool about six inches in front of the left leg of the chair. Sit well to the front of the chair and place your left foot on the footstool. The left thigh should now be slightly angled up from the hip to the knee, and it is this angle which is so critical in the positioning of the guitar. If the thigh is not angled sufficiently, raise the footstool to the next setting. The right thigh should preferably be angled down very slightly, and it may be necessary to push the right foot back and under the chair a little to achieve this, resting on the ball of the foot only. The important thing is balance. In figure 2 the left leg is taking all the strain

which causes a build up of tension. Sit up straight, (this is also beneficial for breathing) and place the guitar waist flat on your left thigh. You will notice that the angling of the thigh causes the guitar to slant backwards slightly – this is intentional – projection of sound is better, also a small space is created between the back of the guitar and the player, which allows the wood to vibrate freely.

Don't try to hug the guitar in to your body, this will upset the angling effect, tending to slant the guitar forward instead, which means the player will have to lean forward to see the fingerboard, so putting a great deal of strain on the back and neck muscles. By having the guitar tilted backwards slightly, the player can sit up straight so that all the weight is transmitted down the spine, and is not transferred to the arms and shoulders. Also, there is no problem with seeing what is going on in the left hand, and it does away with the need to hang one's head over the fingerboard – the head is very heavy, and once again the strain on the neck muscles is incredible.

This may all sound highly medical but it is absolutely crucial. Sitting properly, the player is very relaxed, and the guitar is supported firmly at four places; the inside of the right leg, the left thigh, by the weight of the right arm on the upper bout, and against the chest. The neck of the guitar should be held at about a 35 to 40 degree angle to the ground, so that the head of the instrument is on a level with your shoulder. Figure 3 shows my playing position.

fig.2

fig.3

3 POSITION OF THE RIGHT ARM AND HAND

The right arm should rest on the edge of the guitar body at approximately the widest point – that is, in line with, or fractionally below, the bridge. On which part of the forearm the edge of the guitar comes into contact will vary from person to person, but a useful yardstick is that the shorter the arm, the nearer one must rest to the elbow.

A good way of checking this arm position – and also for setting up the right hand position – is to hold the guitar as stated earlier, and place the right hand flat on the strings over the lower or bridge side of the sound-hole, so that the base of the first three fingers comes approximately over the third, second, and first strings, (figure 5). Now raise the hand by arching the wrist, and at the same time straighten the fingers. Remember to have the forearm resting in line with, or just behind, the bridge. If the wrist is too high, flatten it slightly by drawing the right arm back a little, resting on the guitar edge a little further from the elbow. Finally, turn the right hand from the wrist fractionally towards the bridge which will bring it into the correct playing position. If the position of the right arm is still not correct, it may be because the angle at which you are holding the guitar has been altered. Check this again: if the angle of the guitar neck is too low the arm will be resting too far from the bridge (round towards the end of the guitar body) and if too high then your arm could even end up resting in the waist of the instrument.

Fig. 5

Here then is a quick run down of what has been discussed so far: Sit well to the front on a good solid chair, with the left foot on a footstool set to such a height that the left thigh slopes upward from the hip, with the right thigh sloping down a little. Keeping your back straight, and not letting your head hang down, place the guitar across your left thigh, so that the guitar head is at about the same height as your shoulders. The angle of the strings and guitar neck should now be at about 35 or 40 degrees to the ground, with the guitar tilted back very slightly. Place the right hand, palm down, across the strings at the lower edge of the sound-hole, with the base of the first three fingers resting on strings 3, 2, and 1. Rest the right arm lightly on the guitar front so that it meets the edge a fraction below the bridge. Next, arch the wrist, at the same time straightening the fingers so that they are approximately at right-angles to the back of the hand. Now relax

the fingers and let them hang so that they are slightly curved. Turn the hand a little towards the bridge. The right wrist, with the hand in the normal playing position should be gently arched. Any feeling of strain or tension usually means that the arching is too high. If there is difficulty in striking the bass strings (4, 5, and 6) with the thumb, it may be because the wrist is too low. (This last point should also be checked when you have grown your thumb nail to a reasonable length.) It is a matter of the hand determining where the arm should rest, not the other way about, so if the wrist must be lowered , this should be achieved by drawing the right arm back and resting further down the forearm from the elbow.

Fig. 6

You should now have a hand position similar to that in figure 6. The majority of guitarists play with the third finger at right angles to the strings, the middle finger leaning slightly forward, and the index finger leaning still more, (figure 7). If, however, you have a very short third finger, or a long thumb, it may be to your advantage to play with the middle finger, or even the index finger at right angles if the situation demands it. The main thing is evenness in the right hand, with no bouncing to interrupt this. Notice how the thumb is held outside the fingers. You can test the position for yourself in the following way. Place the thumb on string six, index finger on string three, middle finger on string two,

Fig. 7

and third finger on string one. Don't try and play anything. Make sure the thumb comes into contact with the string about an inch to an inch-and-a-half in front of the index finger, so forming a cross (figure 8). It is only in certain special effects that the thumb moves inside the line of the fingers.

The length of the thumb also has an effect on the height of the wrist. It is the placement of the thumb which matters, and the wrist may have to be lowered a little if your thumb is particularly short. People with long thumbs may have to end up tilting the hand as mentioned earlier, as there is a limit to how high the wrist can be held before the tendons in the hand and wrist become strained. The classical guitar, more than any other instrument, I would say, is highly personal.

I hope I have not bored you with this long dissertation on right hand positioning, but it cannot be stressed enough how terribly important basic technique like this really is. Time spent now sorting out all these points will make an enormous difference later on when it comes to clarity, volume, tone colour, and last but by no means least, speed.

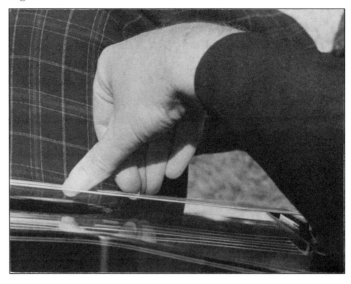

Fig. 8

4 PLUCKING ACTION OF THE RIGHT HAND

For normal playing this consists of two methods: the *free stroke* (sometimes called tirando), and the *rest stroke* (apoyando). I prefer to start pupils off with the free-stroke, and do not agree with teaching a pupil both techniques at the same time as it frequently leads to confusion. I have always believed in developing a strong free stroke attack, only introducing the rest stroke at a later stage for its possibilities in tone colour and accentuation.

With the free stroke, the movement of the tips of the fingers and thumb is circular, or more precisely, elliptical. It is probably easiest to think of the plucking action as a pulling motion, (as against a pushing motion in the case of a rest stroke) beginning the stroke a fraction of an inch from the string, the end joint of the finger or thumb being kept fairly tense. Firstly it is the flesh of the finger tip which makes contact. This acts as a deadening device and also prepares the way for the nail following immediately behind which actually plucks the string, so producing the note. If a vibrating string did not first make contact with the flesh, but went directly onto the nail, a rattle or buzz would be heard at the moment of impact. Figs. 9a, b and c.

Fig. 9(a)

After the string has been plucked, the finger tip will naturally follow-through a short distance because of the power and speed generated in sounding the string. At the end of this follow through, the finger tip then begins its elliptical movement back to a position approximately over the string, or even further round if that string has to be plucked again immediately; in which case the finger returns to its original starting position, a fraction of an inch from the string, ready to attack the next note.

Try to picture this plucking movement of the fingers as starting in the knuckles and going in towards the palm of the hand. In fact, if the action was continued, we would end up with a clenched fist.

The plucking action of the thumb is in one way similar to that of the fingers in that the tip moves in a small ellipse. The difference however is that the thumb does not bend, the movement for the stroke coming from the base of the thumb, not from the hand or arm.

It was stated earlier that the hand is turned from the wrist towards the bridge to bring it into a playing position. This, if carried too far, could lead to the fingers plucking at right angles to the strings – what I call playing "square on". This results usually in a thin tone, and also clicking caused by the string in its progression from finger tip to nail becoming caught in the "valley" between the two. The strings are better plucked with the hand placed slightly off the right-angled position (figure 10). This will result in a warmer, fuller, and clearer sound.

Fig. 9(b)

Fig. 9(c)

Fig. 10

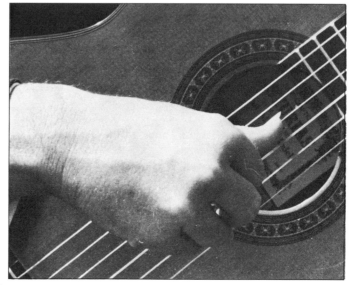

Concert performers these days use either the left or right side of the finger nail. The left side technique is favoured by most performers, being used by celebrated names such as Julian Bream, John Williams, and Alirio Diaz. The right side method came to the fore largely through the superb playing of the late Ida Presti. Both methods work perfectly well, and a number of concert performers, myself included, have incorporated both into their techniques. However, I must once again for the purposes of this book make a decision as to which one I would suggest, and therefore advise the reader to try the left-side technique to begin with. Just in case you are in any doubt about which is the left side of the nail, please study figure 11.

One tip I can give is to those whose index fingers bend inwards. Here I would suggest you experiment using the right corner of the nail, as the finger bends naturally in that direction. To go back to an earlier point: right side playing requires a more pronounced bending or twisting of the wrist towards the bridge. If any pain is experienced, stop, as serious damage can result. Some people find it difficult, even impossible to turn the wrist that far, and to these I would say persevere with the left-side method, as far less strain and tension is created.

Fig. 11

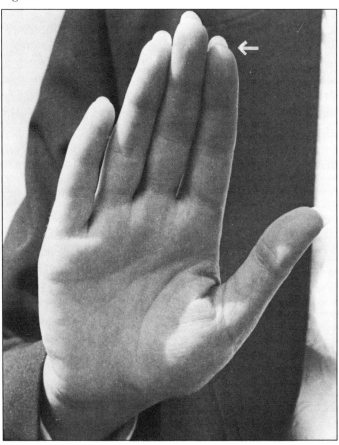

5 TUNING THE GUITAR

Tuning can be a difficult procedure to begin with, but like anything else in life it becomes easier with practice. It is simply a matter of training the ear. A tuning fork of course only produces one note, so what system do we use for tuning all the other strings? This method is to tune the first string from the tuning fork, then gradually working across the remaining five strings using the first as a reference to start the process.

There are two very important "do nots" which must be made clear:
1. Do not tune the open first string to the same pitch as the tuning fork, (open string meaning when it is not being depressed with a left hand finger at one of the frets). To try and get this string up to A = 440 would be asking for trouble. The least that will happen is the string will break; at worst, the bridge will start lifting up, or the neck start bending!
2. Do not slacken the strings off every night. It just is not necessary, and in fact to do so would be harmful to the guitar, because of the constantly changing stresses on the front. If however you are not going to be playing on the guitar for several weeks or months, it is advisable to take the tension off the strings.

The correct tuning procedure is as follows: sound the tuning fork by striking one of its prongs on your knee. The prongs are now vibrating, but it is difficult to hear because the sound is hardly being amplified. To do this, place the end of the tuning fork gently on the side of the guitar fingerboard (figure 12). You will immediately hear the note A, (440 vibrations per second.) Now press the first string, (the one furthest away from you when holding the guitar in the playing position), *just behind* the fifth fret, using the middle finger of the left hand. Don't worry too much about the technique for the moment, just press with the finger tip, and try to get the left thumb approximately under the same fret, but in the middle of the neck (figure 13). This note (string e, fret 5) should be tuned to produce the same note as

the tuning fork, by adjusting the geared machine head, either raising or lowering the pitch of the string accordingly.

Once the first string is in tune, the second string is tuned by pressing it down also at the fifth fret, and adjusting the pitch so that it sounds the same as the open first string. The third string is tuned in a similar manner, except that it should be depressed at fret *four* – this note tuned to sound the same as the open second string. The fourth, fifth, and sixth strings are all tuned at fret five, being pitched against the open third, fourth, and fifth strings respectively. Keeping the guitar at exactly the correct pitch is terribly important. To begin with, the student must accustom himself to the sound of a correctly tuned guitar, and the guitar itself has to be played in, which is best thought of as like the running in of a car. The top or front gradually starts responding to certain frequencies, and if the whole pitch of the instrument is constantly shifting, this process becomes altered.

For those who own a piano which is kept at correct pitch, follow the procedure outlined above but instead of tuning initially to the note A, tune the *open* first string to E (the one lying directly above middle C on the keyboard). If in doubt, ask somebody to show you. Eventually, those with pianos will have to invest in a tuning fork, for the time will come when you will be taking the guitar to other people's houses, and guitars unfortunately do not stay in tune very long. Indeed, I have found that in concerts, from leaving the artist's room and going to the platform, having perhaps walked only twenty yards down a draughty corridor, the guitar has gone completely out of tune! So please have patience with the poor soloist who appears to be tinkering around and wasting time before the first piece. It is better this than the horribly out of tune playing I have heard on occasion, even in major concert halls!

Fig. 13

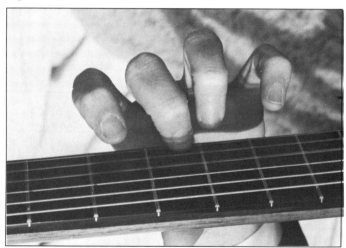

Fig. 12

6 THE NAILS, AND HOW TO LOOK AFTER THEM

To me the most important thing in playing the classical guitar is to produce a beautiful tone. There is of course one very important factor determining tone quality, and that is the correct use and care of the right hand nails.

Firstly, why should we bother using nails at all? It is true that many of the guitarists of past eras did not use nails, they simply plucked the strings with their finger tips. Now, a number of factors must be considered. In earlier times, guitarists were only expected to play in music rooms, salons, ballrooms, chapels, small theatres, etc., where the lower volume level they produced did not matter. It is difficult to compare this with the vast numbers one has to play to these days, sometimes in large concert halls with not always the kindest of acoustics. Today the concert performer must produce a sound which, without the aid of electronic amplification, will project to even the back row of a hall holding 1000, 2000, or even 3000 people.

The theory was that if the nails were used, the tone quality could never be as sweet and as pure as that produced with just the finger tip. It took until the beginning of the 20th century for nail playing to become established, largely through the untiring efforts of Andrés Segovia, regarded by many as the greatest exponent of the instrument (figure 14). Today it is used by just about every concert guitarist, and it is now the generally accepted way of sounding the strings, being taught by certainly 99% of teachers around the world. When properly executed it produces a very clear, balanced sound, with a greater dynamic level, and a wider range of tone colour.

As has been stated in an earlier chapter, the attack should not be at exactly 90 degrees to the string, but slightly angled, producing a smoother transition as the string moves from the finger tip on to the nail. It is the nail which actually produces the note, the quality and texture of sound being determined by the degree of angling of the attack. An important point must be made clear here. The further from the 90 degree position you attack the strings, the greater the risk of string noise, (the nail sliding along the covered strings) and also nail wear. There is a narrow arc in which the nail will produce a good clear attack, and it is up to each individual student to work out his or her own way of achieving this by experimentation.

There are no hard and fast rules for nail length; it is also connected with the point raised at the end of the last paragraph and is a matter of experimentation. With the right hand turned so that the palm is facing you, it should be possible to see the tip of the first, second, and third finger nails over the ends of the fingers (the little finger is not used, except by a few concert players and even then very rarely). The visible part of the nail can vary from as little as a millimetre to three or even four mm in extreme cases. As many of you will not have long nails to begin with, I would suggest you try them 1 mm. and then 2 mm. to see how they work. The thumb nail is of course also used, and I would suggest 2 – 3 mm as a good length to begin with, going up to 5 or 6 mm if need be. In only a few cases would I recommend a longer nail. A long nail is inclined to flex more, so reducing power. Once there is some nail visible, this must be gently filed to produce the correct contour. Never cut the nails with scissors, always use a good quality nail file, or failing that, a fine grade emery board. Take any jagged edges and corners, and try shaping each nail

rather like a crescent moon (Figure 15). If the nails hook over, (bend inwards) a flatter profile often works well.

Once the nail is the correct shape, the edge must be smoothed with very fine grade wet and dry paper, obtainable from a hardware or tool shop. Use grade 800, or better still 1200. Polish the tip and just inside the tip of the nail. Finally, bring the nail tip to a glass finish, rub with an ordinary pencil eraser or an old piece of leather. A smooth nail produces a smooth sound!

For those with weak nails, there may be a vitamin deficiency in the diet, in which case a course of calcium tablets, or bonemeal may help. Gelatine is also worth trying if the nails are brittle. However, nail hardeners are very often the only answer. There are now several very good products available from chemists, and even an excellent nail tonic made especially for guitarists called Tuff Nail of which I have heard good reports. None of these will work miracles in a few days. It may be weeks, even months before a change can be detected. In the case of something like calcium, the period can be anything from three to seven months depending on how quickly that the individual's nails grow.

If after all methods of strengthening have been tried, your nails are still dropping off when you breathe on them, it may be necessary to resort to artificial nails. Again, try different brands as they can vary quite a bit, and always follow the instructions. It has been found that the best results are obtained if the adhesive recommended by the manufacturer is applied first to your own nail then left to dry for a few moments before the artificial nail, (also with the adhesive applied) is positioned.

I hope these comments will help; with badly shaped and unpolished nails, the guitar can sound awful. Take a little time each day to give your nails the once over, it really is worth it!

Fig. 15

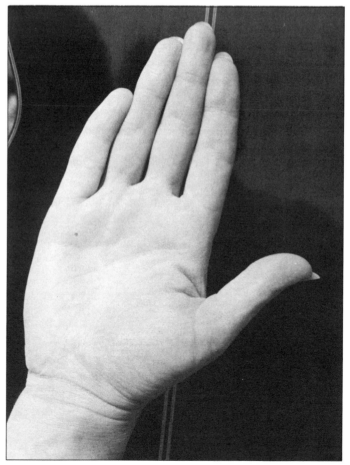

7 OPEN STRING PLAYING

Having tuned the guitar correctly, and checked that you are sitting in the recommended manner, it is now time to start the serious business of playing.

The guitar is a wonderful instrument in that an absolute beginner can make a pleasant sound almost immediately. Unlike many other instruments which require weeks or even months of struggling with the basic technicalities to produce a good sound, the guitar responds straight away to the touch of even the most untrained hand.

The first playing we will be doing involves only the right hand. It is difficult enough for a beginner to try and locate the correct strings, (and this can be a very real problem for the first few days) without the added complications of left-hand fingering. We are going to concern ourselves for the time being with making a nice sound using only the open strings. Much space has been devoted to the discussion of the position and plucking action of the right hand, so now it is a matter of putting the machinery into operation.

Having checked your posture and right hand position, pluck the first string with the index finger. Make sure the middle finger does not move in sympathy with it. Do this several times slowly, trying to move the finger tips in that elliptical path discussed in an earlier chapter. The thumb and other two fingers should be held above the strings (figure 16).

Next, play the same string several times alternating between index and middle fingers, a good speed being about one note per second. It is suggested that several minutes be spent on this little exercise so that you are sure about the basic plucking action of the fingers, before going on to the next exercise in which different strings are introduced. Try to keep the fingers moving smoothly and continuously and don't jab at the strings. Aim at having the finger which is not playing (but is at that moment returning to its former position) passing approximately over the string when the other finger is executing its plucking movement. This may sound complicated, but in simple terms the fingers should pass each other approximately in the middle of their stroke.

The next exercise is similar to the last, except that the second and third strings are now brought into play. Start on the first string by playing it four times; index, middle, index, middle, one note per second. After the fourth note move without a break to the second string and repeat the process, then continue on to the third string. The exercise can be rounded off by playing the second and then the first strings again, each four times. So our exercise is as follows:–

1st String	–	index	middle	index	middle
2nd String	–	"	"	"	"
3rd String	–	"	"	"	"
2nd String	–	"	"	"	"
1st String	–	"	"	"	"

Whilst playing, always be checking on your posture and the movement of the fingers. When crossing over from the first string to the lower strings, the right hand must be turned a little more from the wrist towards the bridge. This is because the line of the

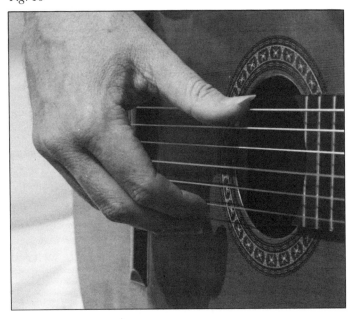

Fig. 16

forearm is being pushed at a shallower angle to the strings as the right hand works its way across towards the bass strings, (4, 5, and 6) and there must be some compensation to ensure the right hand fingers are still attacking the strings at the correct angle (figure 17). Doing this will produce a clearer, less scratchy tone, and also reduce nail wear.

Fig. 17

To round off this chapter: when we come to reading printed guitar music, the right hand fingering is often indicated, and naturally some sort of abbreviated form is called for. The early editions from the 19th century in particular used a system of dots and crosses, but this was confusing at times and rather untidy. A new and improved system has now been generally accepted using as a starting point the Spanish names for the thumb and fingers, and simply taking the first letters of each. In the table printed below, the Spanish names appear in brackets.

p = thumb (pulgar)		i = index finger (indice)	
m = middle finger (medio)		a = third finger (anular)	

8 FIRST STEPS IN READING MUSIC

Now that you have begun to play the guitar, it is essential to know the notes you are playing. Music is written on five lines called a stave (example 1).

Example 1

At the beginning of the stave is a clef sign. In the case of guitar music the treble clef is used.

The clef determines the pitch of the notes in relation to the five lines of the stave. In the case of the treble or G clef, the second line from the bottom of the stave passes through the middle of the large loop of the letter G, this line always represents a note of G. In fact, the letter G is the furthest point reached in the alphabet in terms of musical notation, after G the whole sequence begins again with the letter A.

For now let us concern ourselves with the notes which lie within the boundaries of the stave. They all appear in example 2.

Example 2

In example 3 I have separated the nine notes into those which lie on the lines of the stave, and those which sit in the spaces.

Example 3

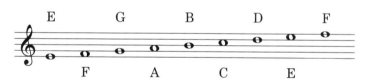

To help you remember the notes on the lines, it is customary to make up a sentence using these letters to begin each word. For example, "Every Good Boy Deserves Favours". For the notes in the spaces, these letters make up the word FACE, very easily remembered. The first three strings of the guitar are all tuned to notes lying within the range of the stave.

They are:

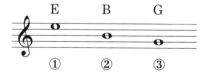

(The numbers below the notes indicate the string, and are always circled in this way.)

Note values tell us how long each note should sound in relation to the speed or tempo of the piece. The starting point here is the *whole note* which appears at the top of example 4. Below that are two *half notes*, each one literally half the value of the whole note, and these in turn can each be split in half to make *quarter notes*.

Example 4

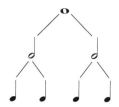

Some teachers prefer to use the older names for these notes,

easily remembered system of half notes, etc.

Music is divided into BARS, each one ending with a bar line, see example 5.

Example 5

Each bar has a fixed number of beats determined by the *time signature* which appears at the beginning of the piece, or sometimes part of the way through a piece at the beginning of a new section. The top figure gives the number of beats in each bar, and the lower figure the value of each beat. So the time signature of $\frac{3}{2}$ would mean three beats in each bar, each beat being worth one half note. A time signature of $\frac{4}{4}$ means four quarter notes to each bar, and so on. The exercise we learnt in the last chapter would then be written as follows:

Exercise 1.

There are four quarter notes to each bar; notice also how it is customary to conclude any section or piece of music with a double bar line. Let us now play this piece once again, but at the end, an extra bar will be added in which we play the first string *once* but let it ring for *four* beats – in other words making it a whole note. The small noughts against certain notes mean open string, and as each note is played several times, it is not necessary to write them in every time. When you play the final note count to yourself four beats, and hold it for the correct duration, (the count of 1 coming at the same time as the note).

Exercise 1b.

Right hand fingering

9 MORE OPEN-STRING EXERCISE

The three top strings of the guitar should now be becoming familiar to you, after learning exercise 1b in the last chapter. Our next piece appears below. The notes used in this, and also in exercise 3, are exactly the same as in 1b, so there are no problems in finding notes here. One thing which is different is the time signature which you will notice is $\frac{3}{4}$ three quarter-notes to each bar, in other words three beats each worth one quarter-note.

Let us look for any 'problem' bars which may crop up.

Exercise 2.

The first three bars are very straightforward, but bar 4 has a different value note. In it we have a half-note (2 beats), but notice the dot placed after it. This dot lengthens the note by half its value, so that it is now worth *three* quarter-note beats. This is called a dotted half-note. A similar thing occurs in the last bar of the piece.

This might be an appropriate time to deal with a problem concerning right-hand fingering. Many tutor books stipulate a rigid fingering system whereby the first string is always plucked with the *a* finger, the second string with the *m* finger, and so on. This system has now fallen out of use, as it is really not very practical, particularly in pieces requiring any degree of speed. To maintain a smooth flow in scales or passages of repeated notes, alternate fingers must be used in the right hand.

One final point with exercise No. 2, at the end there is the following sign:

This indicates that the piece is to be repeated from the beginning. Sometimes in the middle of a piece we get the following:

this means that this particular section must be repeated. By the way, don't forget *a* = third finger. The speed of this little piece should be quite relaxed, perhaps just a shade quicker than exercise 1b.

To conclude this chapter here is one final open string study using the top three strings. The most important thing to concentrate on here is the counting, particularly in bars 5 and 9. The time signature may seem rather curious. Basically it means the same as $\frac{4}{4}$ and has come to be known, (although technically speaking, incorrectly) as Common Time. You need to become acquainted with it as you will encounter this time signature frequently. The history behind it is most interesting for it shows that today we have come to accept what is in fact a misconception of the real meaning of this sign. Many centuries ago the time signatures that were in use were basically in the shape of the Circle, indicating "perfect" time (triple – what today we would regard as having three beats in the bar,) and a Semi-circle for "imperfect" time (duple – two or four beats.) Over the years the rather ornate semi-circle has become a capital letter *C*, which many regard as standing for Common Time, although as we see, it originates from a now obsolete way of indicating time values. As to the piece, begin by playing it at one note per second. When learnt, you may like to take it at about double this speed.

Exercise 3.

10 THE REST STROKE (APOYANDO)

Having dealt with the free stroke thoroughly, we shall now turn our attention to the rest stroke which, because of its slightly fuller and more sonorous tone quality, is the technique used mainly for scales and melodic passages.

The reason it is called a rest stroke is because after striking the string each finger goes through and rests for a fraction of a second on the next string down. My opinion is that there must be two sorts of rest stroke, one for scale and single note melodic playing, and the other kind for isolated notes in chordal or arpeggiated (broken chord) passages. In the former the fingers are held a little straighter than for the free stroke, and it may be necessary to draw the knuckles of the hand back slightly, across towards the lower strings, at the same time tilting the hand slightly towards the sound hole with all three fingers leaning in that direction (figure 18), so compensating for the difference in length between the index and middle fingers. I hasten to add that this method would be employed if only the *i* and *m* fingers were to be used. If the *a* finger were involved, then a more upright position should be adopted. Because of the angling of the fingers, there may be no need to use the widely taught practice of collapsing the first joint which can easily lead to trouble, for one theory is that pronounced collapsing is a delaying factor, and as far as scales are concerned we are aiming eventually at some degree of pace (figure 19).

With the second type of rest stroke the hand should remain more or less in the same position as for free stroke playing, which then means that certainly the middle finger and possibly all three fingers should collapse at the first joint when executing this rest stroke, as there simply is not time to alter the hand position, and this is the only way the finger nail can produce a downward stroke, at the attack (figure 20). So to clarify that, in scales try to avoid any collapsing, but for isolated notes some degree of collapsing is required to use a rest stroke. For both methods, the movement begins from the knuckle, and is best thought of as a downward pushing motion so that for the first part of the stroke the finger acts as one unit. On the return to its starting point, the first and second joints come into play, and as with the free stroke, the finger tip travels in an ellipse.

This may all sound highly technical and advanced, and some of the information does not really apply to you right now. However, I would suggest you make a mental note to study this chapter again and in greater depth at a later date, say several months from now, when you should be tackling scales and right hand studies containing isolated rest strokes. For now, practise this new technique using exercises 1b, 2, and 3, which you have already learnt. (I would suggest the non-collapsing variety be used for the moment.)

Fig. 18

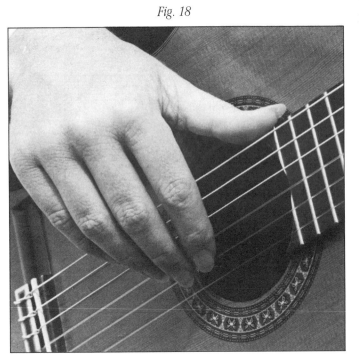

Fig. 19

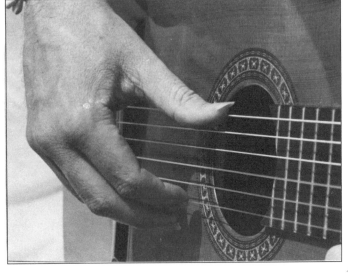

Fig. 20

11 THE OPEN BASS STRINGS

When looking at the way the 4th, 5th, and 6th strings are written, you will notice that all three come below the stave.

Example 6.

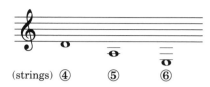

(strings) ④ ⑤ ⑥

The fourth string (D) comes immediately below the lowest line of the stave. For notes beneath this, we must use extra short lines to represent an extension of the stave. These are called *leger lines*, and are also used above the normal stave as well. Our fifth string (A) lies on the second leger line down, and the sixth string (E) comes underneath the third leger line. For the moment we are going to pluck all three strings with the thumb, although in more advanced pieces, and scales, the fingers are also used on the bass string. First practise using free strokes, and then rest strokes. As with the fingers, the tip of the thumb moves in an ellipse, but for rest strokes the first joint is always collapsed.

Exercise 4.

Exercise 5.

12 PIECES USING ALL SIX OPEN STRINGS

Having learnt to use the three bass strings, now is the time to combine these with the treble strings. Not only are we now playing across all six strings, there is also the problem of using thumb and fingers of the right hand in the same piece.

A comment here about the way guitar music is written. Up to now the various exercises have been written as single note melodies. Most music for the instrument has several parts of voices going on at the same time. In these next pieces you will see how the music is divided into treble and bass parts, the treble notes having their stems pointing upwards, and the bass notes having their stems pointing downwards.

There are places where notes are missing in one or other of the parts, and here these must be filled up with rests. The rests are shown in the following table placed on the same line as their corresponding note values for easy reference.

In the same way as a dot after a note increases its value by half, so the same applies to rests, e.g.

$$ \text{(image)} = \text{♩.} \left(\text{♩} + \text{♪} \right) $$

A good example of rests can be seen in Exercise 6. In the top part there is a quarter note rest on the first beat of each bar, and for the last two bars, only the bass is sounding, so the full three beats must be filled out with rests in each bar. One other point, notice that the last two bass notes are joined by a curved line. This is called a *tie*. When two notes of the same pitch are connected in this way, the first note is the only one which is actually played. It is then held for the duration of the two notes combined, in this case two dotted half-notes or a total of six beats. A general comment about guitar pieces written in this style is that the treble notes are normally intended to continue sounding for longer than

Fig. 21

their written value. It would be confusing to write this as the page would become a mass of tie-lines and be very difficult to read. In Exercise 6 for example, the first quarter note in each bar would not be stopped, and the second one (3rd beat) would continue sounding through the first beat of the next bar where the rest appears.

A final word about right hand technique before you play Exercise 6. The way in which the finger-tips move smoothly in an elliptical path on their return to their original position, also applies to the thumb. In the first bar, try to bring the tip of the thumb back smoothly, (moving the thumb from the third joint), whilst the index and third fingers are striking the strings (figure 21).

Exercise 6.

Notice how when a string is missed out, the right-hand fingering compensates – in the above exercise in bars 1, 3, 5, and 6 there is no 2nd string, so no middle finger. This is of great importance, particularly later on in chord playing.

The second piece in this chapter introduces eighth-notes. These are written as follows: ♪ for single notes, but where two or more are grouped together they usually appear as : ♫ The value of the eighth-note is half that of a quarter note. The corresponding rests look like this: ♇ and they appear in almost every bar of this next piece. Do not forget about the repeats, and check to make sure you are using the correct right hand fingering. Remember the right hand position, with the thumb outside the fingers and do not let the wrist get too low. Listen to your sound, and try to make each note clear, with a good balance over all six strings, using free-strokes throughout.

Exercise 7.

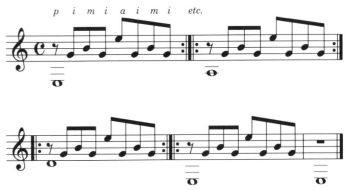

13 LEFT HAND POSITION AND FINGERING

Guitar playing is in many ways a very curious business because of the strange contortions we frequently impose on ourselves both with right and left hands, and even the best basic posture is not exactly conducive to incredibly good health! We are making the hands do things they were never intended to do in normal living, very often using muscles we have not used since the early weeks of our lives.

Fig. 22

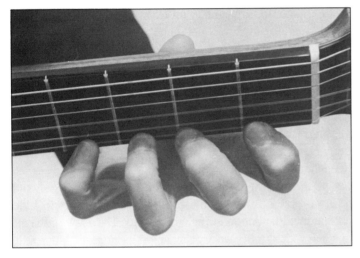

The basic position of the left hand is with the fingers curled, and the thumb held straight so that the ball of the thumb comes approximately mid-way between 1st and 2nd fingers (figure 22). By the way, to avoid any confusion with the right hand, we shall be referring to the left hand fingers as one, two, three, and four, starting with the index finger. Try doing this away from the guitar at first just to get the hand used to this movement. The thumb, in relation to the fingers, will naturally vary from person to person, and a good check is to make a fist with your left hand, and observe where the *first joint* of the thumb lies. In many cases it will come in line with the second finger, or between the first and second fingers. A few people find it best to have the thumb under the index finger, or even as far ahead as the third finger, but these are fairly rare cases.

You may have noticed that with the fingers held in the position described above, the back of the left hand and the forearm feel more comfortable if held in more or less a straight

Fig. 23

line. Any effort to push the wrist in or out puts strain on the tendons, and restricts movement of the fingers. This "straight line" theory is actually carried further, because the knuckles of the four fingers should also be in line with the back of the hand and forearm. The middle joint of the fingers should be at about right-angles to this line, and the first joint almost parallel to the knuckles, (figure 23). Now, this is just a starting point to illustrate the very, very basic position, but some time should be devoted to getting the hand accustomed to this seemingly rather strange position, and generally getting the fingers loosened up. Before going on to the next exercise, make sure your left hand nails are cut nice and short.

When this position is transferred to the fingerboard, it all suddenly makes sense. The idea is to press the strings down just behind the frets using the *tips* of the finger to impart a degree of pressure sufficient to produce a clear note. Do not press too hard, or strain in any way, pressing either on, or too far away from the frets gives a muffled note, or a buzz, respectively. Try the following little exercise: Press the four fingers down on string no. 1; the first finger at fret seven, second finger at fret eight, third at fret nine, and fourth at fret ten. The reason for playing high up the fingerboard is because the frets are closer together and create less of a problem for the hand. Remember to press only with the finger tip, making sure there is daylight between all the fingers. The third is particularly weak and very often wants to rest on the

Fig. 24

second finger so make a special effort to separate these two fingers. Indeed, fingers 2 and 3 are the only ones which meet the string in a vertical position. The first finger lies slightly on its side, and the fourth finger also lies slightly on its side, but in the opposite direction (figure 24).

Keep the thumb straight, and bent backwards at the tip joint. Rest the ball of the thumb approximately in the middle of the neck, in line with the second finger, or wherever is most comfortable, (as explained earlier). The thumb must never protrude above the neck, as this pushes the rest of the hand out of position. In classical guitar playing the thumb is not normally used to depress a string. Do not allow the palm of the hand to touch the edge of the fingerboard, as this will impair the movement of the fingers. It is most important to hold all four fingers absolutely parallel to the strings, so that you press with the *middle* of the tip of each finger. Another guide to help you here is to have the back of the hand parallel to the edge of the fingerboard. To explain why we attach so much importance to this, if the hand were allowed to turn side on in any way (figure 25), the little finger would be hopelessly out of distance. Secondly, it is more difficult to press the strings down cleanly with an angled left hand position and there is a risk of the string being pushed out of tune if it is not depressed straight down.

Fig. 25

Remember to keep the tip segments of the fingers upright, and try to feel the string being squeezed between thumb and finger tip, (the theory here is more strength with less effort!). Do not have the elbow pulled in so that it actually touches the side of your body, or pushed too far out. Just let the left arm and hand relax naturally.

The next exercise is one which involves carrying the fingers across towards the bass strings, in fact it is a kind of 'walking' exercise. There is no right hand, so one can concentrate on left hand finger movement. Starting as we did just now, press the left hand fingers down on the first string beginning at fret seven with first finger, then second finger fret eight, third finger fret nine, and fourth finger fret ten. Once a finger has gone down keep it on the string until it is needed again. Keeping fingers two, three and four on the first string, put the 1st finger on to the second string at fret seven. Follow with the 2nd, then the 3rd, and finally the 4th fingers. Continue in this way, gradually working across towards the 6th string. Having reached the point where all four fingers have been placed on the 6th string, begin working back over towards the top string. This exercise will help give strength and independence to the fingers.

A very important point is that in moving from the treble to the bass strings, the wrist must be pushed further out. This is achieved *not* by moving the thumb further round underneath the neck, but by rolling across the ball of the thumb (in fact pivoting might be a better way to describe this), so that you end up resting on the *inside* edge of the first joint (figure 26). When coming back from bass to treble, this movement is of course reversed. On the bass strings, the left hand fingers will be more gently curved in profile, but still always pressing down on the finger tips.

Fig. 26

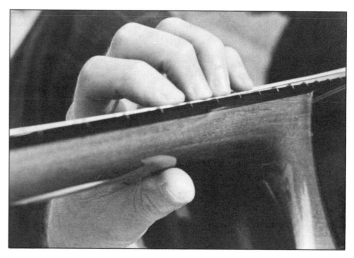

To close, here are some points to look out for whilst practising this finger-independence exercise. Try to keep the hand still, and don't reach for notes by turning the wrist or angling the hand. Keep the fingers spread apart, and always remember to press just behind the frets. At this position on the fingerboard there should be no problem reaching any of the notes, with the possible exception of the bottom string which may cause a few problems to begin with. If so, practise going across as far as the fifth string. It is not absolutely crucial to cover all six strings at the moment, and as long as you can reach as far as the fifth string comfortably, this is fine. Always think of moving the fingers, *not* the hand. The fingers should move up and down like hammers, but be careful not to lift them too high – about half-an-inch at the most. The fingers must always remain bent as this automatically restricts the height they can be lifted from the fingerboard, the movement coming from the knuckles (figure 27). When you see a top class performer in action, one is always aware of how easy the piece is made to look. Economy of movement is the secret, (and this applies to the right hand as well!). The smaller the movements of the fingers, the less risk there is of making a mistake, and most importantly the music can be allowed to flow easily and smoothly, for after all, technique is only a means to an end, and it is above all else the music which is the most important reason for playing.

Fig. 27

14 PRACTISING

I think this is a good time to say a few words on this very important subject, as I have found to my surprise that most students, even some at a very advanced level have never been given any guidance on this matter.

Some of the points I am going to mention may seem very basic, but it is amazing how many people have overlooked them.

1. Always practise alone. It is no good trying to work with somebody else in the room even if they say they are quite happy doing their own thing. Your concentration will be broken frequently, and there always comes the time when the other person comments "is that the only tune you know, that must be thirty times already today you have played it!" The point is, whenever there is another person present, you are always *playing* and not *practising*. Now the two words may appear to describe the same function, but they are totally different. Practice is a highly concentrated process of feeding information into the brain. After much time and effort this becomes firmly established in the sub-conscious and it is a recall process which is put into operation during any performance, whether it be in front of 3000 people in the Royal Festival Hall, London, or members of your family in your front room! Practice and playing cannot be mixed, for it is impossible to give a good performance of something which has not been thoroughly learnt; preferably memorized.

2. Your practice room must be quiet, warm (17˚–20˚ Centigrade), and well ventilated. Cold conditions are hopeless, but on the other hand a stuffy airless room is difficult to concentrate in for any length of time.

3. Always check that your guitar is at the correct pitch before you begin each practice session.

4. Set yourself a goal or target each time you practise, whether it be to learn a certain exercise, a study, or to improve a difficult section from a piece. Never allow idle 'messing around' to creep into the sessions. Even if it is possible to do only half-an-hour on a given day, a fantastic amount can be achieved in that time with the right sort of concentration.

5. Never practise for more than one hour at a time. I know when things are going well it is difficult to put the guitar down, but believe me, even ten minutes' rest will help restore concentration. It has been proved scientifically that the human mind cannot focus for more than a few minutes on any one subject before concentration begins to wander. With training, it is possible to maintain a reasonable level for 45 minutes or even an hour, but after this time the level of concentration has dropped so low, (less than 50% of what we started with), that it is

dangerous to go on, even though we may feel alert. What it amounts to quite simply is that faults, both musical and technical, creep in when we are tired, and these faults especially the latter variety can take months to eradicate.

6. Do not try to cram too much material into one practice session. Divide up the time so that you have a part of the session for technical work, (scales, exercises, etc.) and part for working on a particular piece. A little done well is infinitely preferable to a lot done badly.

7. Listen carefully to your playing all the time. Aim at producing a full, warm, and clear sound, without cutting or clipping any notes. Do not rush; practise everything very slowly to begin with. Only when you feel comfortable with the notes at a slow speed can any thought be given to increasing the tempo. To try and play a piece up to speed too soon only hinders progress, for what you are doing is practising your faults, and in the long run making them worse.

8. When you have a piece worked up and are playing it at about the correct speed, avoid the appalling habit of pausing and having another go at a note or group of notes which may have "gone wrong." Major technical problems should have been sorted out long before (see note No. 7), but human beings are not perfect creatures, and slips happen now and then. Don't stop when this hap-pens, get used to "playing through" your mistakes, because the cardinal sin in music is to interrupt or break the flow or rhythm.

9. Do not tackle anything way beyond your ability, simply because you may have heard it in a recital and you felt like trying it yourself. There is no harm in having the piece filed away on the shelf for future reference, but do try to set a carefully planned practice schedule for yourself with the pieces gradually becoming more difficult over the months rather than attempting to take giant strides.

10. Because the guitar is largely a solitary instrument it is important to get out and meet other players. Guitar societies are the perfect answer, and you will almost certainly meet up with somebody of a similar degree of technical ability with whom you can discuss your playing, repertoire, etc., and even practise duets. Guitarists, more so than most other musicians, are guilty of taking liberties (usually subconsciously) with rhythm and tempo. The frequent rehearsal of duets, or better still trios and quartets will help correct this, as very strict attention must be paid to these aspects in any kind of group performance, and it will be far easier to command a firm control of rhythm in your solo playing once you have done this.

15 NOTES ON THE FIRST STRING

The left hand position has already been discussed in an earlier chapter, so it should now be possible to move on to reading and playing notes in the lower regions of the fingerboard, (i.e. towards the nut.)

The exercise in chapter 13 has the first finger pressing at fret *seven*. In guitar jargon this would be referred to as *position* seven, being determined by the fret at which the *first* finger is pressing, and would be written in the form of Roman numerals, (e.g. VII).

In the following studies the notes we shall be learning are all within the first three frets and in the first position. With guitar music many notes have numbers against them. These refer to the left hand fingers which should be used to depress that particular note, they do *not* indicate the fret.

The frets on the guitar fingerboard are set a half-tone or *semitone* apart. The distance between two notes is referred to as an *interval,* and in this book the semitone is the smallest we shall be dealing with. Two semitones make a whole tone, usually simply called a *tone,* which when transferred to the guitar becomes two notes on the same string, separated by two frets. In music we have the following notes: A B C D E F G. After G we start again by calling the next note A. However, it is necessary to understand that the intervals between these notes vary. The following table shows us that B to C, and E to F are only semitones, whereas all the other intervals are tones.

Example 7.

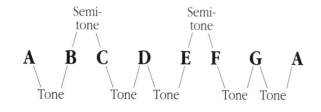

Therefore, if we play the open first string (E) and then play F on the same string, we must press down a semi-tone or *one fret* higher, G being a tone higher than F is found at fret 3.

These then are the notes used in Exercise 8:

Example 8.

The time signature is $\frac{2}{4}$, that is two beats in each bar, each beat being worth one quarter note. *Andante* is a frequently used Italian term which is an indication of the approximate tempo of the piece, in this case moderately slowly, (at about walking pace). The sign over the final note is call a *fermata,* which means that the note in question is to be held a little longer than its written value. Exercise 8 can be practised using rest and free-strokes.

Exercise 8.

16 NOTES ON THE SECOND STRING

Exercise 9 introduces notes on the B or second string. C is a semitone higher than B, so this is played at the first fret, and D being a tone above C is therefore found at fret three.

Example 9.

Andantino is another tempo indication, and is now generally accepted as meaning slightly faster than Andante. "Rit." at the end of this piece is short for *Ritardando,* and means a gradual slowing up, so bringing the music in this case to a satisfactory conclusion. (Another version of this is *Rallentando* which usually appears in its abbreviated form "rall.").

Exercise 9.

As with exercise 8, this can also be practised using free and rest-strokes.

17 PLAYING ON STRINGS ONE, TWO AND THREE

Before going on to Exercise 10, make sure you have practised exercises 8 and 9, so that you are absolutely at home with the new notes on the first and second strings.

Exercise 10.

Exercise 10 is really a right-hand study piece using all three treble strings. The only new note is A on string three. This note is to be found at the second fret, A being a tone above the open string G. In this study, the second finger is used to stop this new note, and all the notes should be played free-strokes making sure you use the thumb for the "bass" notes, (stems pointing downwards). Just before you embark on playing this piece, compare the way the notes are written with Exercise 7. You will notice that the first and fifth notes in every bar, except the final note of the piece, have *two* stems. It would have been just as easy to have written one stem pointing down, with an eighth-note rest over the top, but it is often easier to read if the bass is linked to the treble line by also using an upward pointing stem. *Moderato* is another tempo marking indicating that the speed of the piece or movement is to be taken quite moderately, in fact something a little quicker than Andantino. Don't forget about the slowing up at the end, and to hold the final note on a little longer.

There are several points to check on in this piece. In bar 3 the D is depressed with the fourth finger. This is quite a common fingering for this grouping of notes, and the student should get used to it at this fairly early stage. It also occurs again in bars 6 and 7. In bar 5 we have our new note A, second fret on the third string, but do not forget that the little 2 against the note means finger and not fret. Also, watch out for the change of fingering in the right hand in bar 8.

All the notes of this study also lie within the first three frets on strings, 1, 2, and 3. It would be an idea to study the upper part first, (notes with stems pointing upwards) for by so doing would make the melody familiar to you, and give a strong feeling of the rhythmical flow of the music. Once you feel happy with the

upper part, study the lower part separately. All the notes with stems pointing downwards should be struck with the thumb, (except the final note of the piece, which is part of both treble and bass parts, and is plucked by the index finger). This bass line actually uses only three notes; G (open 3rd string,) A (2nd fret, 3rd string,) and B (open 2nd string). However, the problem is more in the rhythm where in many bars we have the following note pattern;

What is perhaps difficult is that there is no bass note on either the first or third beats of these bars. To practise, try playing and counting as follows:

Count   1 & 2 & 3 &

play

A good practice speed is ♩ = 52, although the piece when learnt might be taken at something around ♩ = 66 – 72.

Exercise 10a.

21

18 CHORD PLAYING USING STOPPED TREBLE STRINGS

The next piece we are going to learn, Exercise 11, is a straight-forward study using the notes already learnt on the treble strings, but incorporating in addition the three open bass strings, D, A, and E. The piece is in three sections, the first stating the basic chords, (groups of notes sounded simultaneously) each one held for a whole bar, (three beats), the second section separating the treble and bass lines so we have a sort of Waltz effect in the rhythm, and thirdly an arpeggio section where each chord is broken or spread out starting with the bass note each time. In section one, try not to 'place' the right hand fingers on the strings before playing each chord, as this will lead to a slight break between the chords. All the notes of a "block" chord must be played free-stroke, sounding exactly together. Also listen to the balance in these chords to make sure no one string drowns out another, and check particularly that the highest note of the chord is audible, as it is the 'a' finger which is involved, probably the weakest finger as far as the majority of people are concerned. Also make sure that the action of thumb and fingers remains that of single note playing, but of course all working together as one unit. In the third section, the same theory applies, that is, the right hand fingers should *not* be placed on the strings before the actual plucking takes place. There are some performers who advise 'planting' as it is called, but I have never been happy about using this method as I honestly believe it leads to bad habits and weaknesses in the right hand. In this arpeggio section, do be careful to not let the 'a' finger move in sympathy with the 'm' finger. Most people to begin with, have this seemingly uncontrollable 'waggle' so that if the middle finger plucks the second string, (as in this

next piece), the 'a' finger goes with it and ends up hopelessly out of position for the next note. A good exercise is the one printed below, which is only for 'm' and 'a' fingers, and I would suggest should be practised before playing exercise 11.

Example 10.

Once again in this next piece, we have the fourth finger pressing down the D on string two. Also be careful in places like bar 4 where the fourth finger lifts off but the first and second remain on. The whole piece should be played free-stroke, with the possible exception of the very last note, which can be played rest-stroke, but here use your ear and judgement. Don't play this note too hard, and use the rest-stroke for its tonal colour, not for accentuation. The marking *allegretto* is again an indication of tempo. This one means reasonably fast, a little quicker than moderato.

Exercise 11.

19 ACCIDENTALS AND TWO NEW NOTES

As we have already found, the interval between the majority of notes (A to B, C to D, etc.,) is that of a tone, but what happens then if we want to play for example a semitone above the note G? We must then use what are called *sharps* and *flats*, which go under the general heading of *accidentals*. A sharp *raises* the note by one semitone, and so G sharp would be written

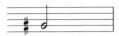

A flat *lowers* the pitch of the note a semitone and is written as follows, ♭. The rule is that if a note is accompanied by an accidental (e.g. G sharp), all other G's *at that same pitch and in the same bar* would also be played sharp. This saves cluttering up the score with masses of accidentals. If however that same G is to return to its normal pitch within that bar, a natural sign must be placed before it. If not, then the sharp sign applies throughout the remainder of the bar, and is only cancelled out by the barline.

In the next piece, "Minuet" by Krieger, we have to play G sharp on the third string at fret one, (a semitone above the open string). There is also another new note to be learnt, E on the fourth string. We know that the interval between D and E is a tone, and moving up from open D we arrive at E on the second fret. The fifth and sixth strings are not used at all in this piece, so you can concentrate on the notes learnt on the top four strings. Do not forget to watch out for the two new notes G sharp and E. On the stave they appear as follows:

Example 11.

Just one more point before we learn the Minuet. At several places in the piece there appear markings such as *p* and *mf*. These are indications of volume, or as it is more often referred to *dynamics*. You will find the following table useful when tackling the rest of the pieces in this book.

pp	*p*	*mp*	*mf*	*f*	*ff*
pianissimo	*piano*	*mezzo piano*	*mezzo forte*	*forte*	*fortissimo*
very soft	soft	moderately	moderately	loud	very loud

When a composer wishes a passage or section to become louder he will put < or simply *crescendo*, while in the case of getting quieter will write > or *decrescendo*, or as it is sometimes called *diminuendo*.

Johann Philipp Krieger, the composer of this Minuet, was born in 1649 and died in 1725. He was German, but received most of his training in Italy. The majority of his output was in the form of Church music, Masses, etc., also operas, and much chamber music. This Minuet comes from one of his smaller keyboard works. The tempo is fairly relaxed, but one must not forget that the piece is basically a dance movement and should therefore have a certain grace of movement rhythmically. I would suggest the first eight bars and the last eight bars be played free-stroke, but that the middle section, (bars 9 to 16), be played rest-stroke. Incidentally, here and in a number of other pieces later on, I have numbered the bars for convenience in locating any problems, etc. The bars are numbered by the following indication:

e.g. ⬚5

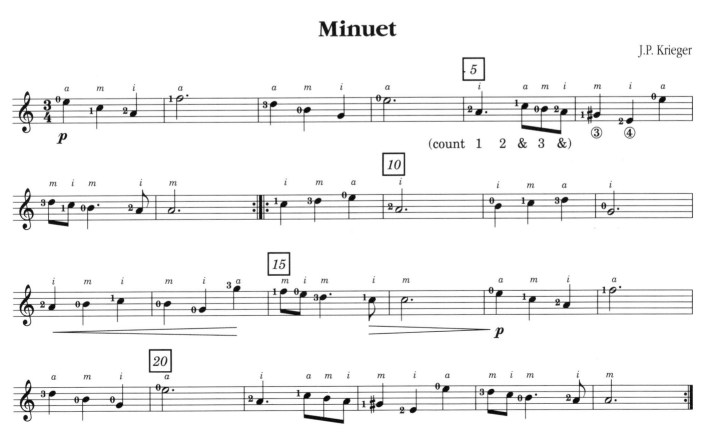

20 SCALE OF C MAJOR, AND KEY SIGNATURES

Before it is possible to play this scale, it will be necessary to learn just two more notes. These are F (4th string, third fret), and C (5th string, third fret).

Example 12.

First let us work out the scale in terms of the left-hand fingering. Below is set out a basic version of the scale of C major. Do not forget that the numbers in circles indicate the string, and the small numbers against the notes represent the left-hand fingers. Also, take note of the right-hand fingering which appears over the top of the notes. Scales are in fact usually played using alternate right-hand fingers, and I would suggest you practise both rest and free-strokes, making sure not to repeat any right hand finger. Do not leave any left-hand fingers down too long, e. g. the 1st note (C) after the D has been sounded. You can however leave fingers on behind other stopped notes *on the same string*, (e.g. E behind F), but don't also put down the first finger as the first fret is not being played, and this is a serious fault which can lead to all sorts of problems. To go back to the E and F, once the G which follows has been plucked, *both* second and third fingers must be lifted off the fourth string. Fingers not in use should be held ready just above the string being played, (figure 28). Smoothness and clarity should be aimed at always.

Scale of C major

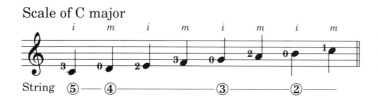

Fig. 28

Having played through the scale several times, it is now important to work out and understand what makes a Major scale. The first note (C) is called the tonic and progressing up the scale, there is a set pattern for the intervals between the notes. This pattern for major scales is always as follows: tone – tone – semitone – tone – tone – tone – semitone. The distance or interval between the first note of the scale, (tonic), and the next note of the same name is an OCTAVE. The following version of the same scale will help you understand these various points a little better.

Example 13.

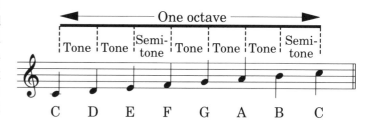

Now, with all these semitones flying about, where are all the sharps and flats? The answer is that there are none in the scale of C Major. To go even further, if the piece we are playing is quite firmly based on this scale, we say it is in the key of C Major. To help us, the composer will put after every treble clef from the beginning of the piece onwards, the key signature, that is the sharps or flats which are associated with the particular scale upon which the piece happens to be based. So with a piece in C Major, there are no accidentals placed at the beginning of the stave.

To continue with our practise of this scale, and to conclude the chapter, I suggest you play the scale both ascending and descending using the following note groups, which will help speed up your right hand. This also introduces sixteenth notes which you will need for the next piece. They are written as follows:

♪ or ♫ and it is probably easiest to think of *two* sixteenths as equalling one eighth note, (♫ = ♪) or *four* sixteenths equalling one quarter note (♬ = ♩). The equivalent rest for the sixteenth note is 𝄿.

When playing on the lower strings with the right hand fingers, it is most important to keep the angle of attack about the same as for the treble strings. This has already been dealt with in the chapter headed "Open String Playing".

In addition to playing scales normally as set out above, it is also possible to work out interesting patterns which not only vary the left-hand fingering, but also make us think a lot more about the right hand because it sometimes is not quite what we expect, particularly in terms of which string we are to play on. Try the following exercises, using rest and free strokes. As before, start with single quarter notes, then eighth notes in pairs, and finally sixteenth notes in groups of four.

Exercise 12

♩=60 (1 quarter note per second)

Exercise 13(a)

Exercise 13(b)

25

21 STUDY IN C MAJOR — CARULLI

At the end of the 18th Century there was a tremendous surge in popularity of the classical guitar which lasted until about the middle of the 19th Century. During this period, a number of names emerged, which have come down to us through the years as being guitarists of very high technical accomplishment who mostly performed their own compositions, (unlike today); and who, almost without exception, were celebrated teachers of the instrument.

As you progress with your studies of the guitar, these names will become familiar: Sor, Giuliani, Carcassi, Aguado, and of course Carulli who is represented in this book by several pleasant and very useful pieces. Ferdinando Carulli was born in Naples in 1770, and died in Paris in 1841. Although one of the earliest players of that period to acquire fame through concerts and teaching, he was in some ways overtaken by others such as Carcassi who emerged a few years later, providing fresh ideas on technique, and bringing before the public more elaborate and dazzling works in concert performances. Carulli however can not be overlooked for he was a very important figure in the development of the guitar at this time and many of his pieces are still used today for teaching purposes, although little of his music is heard on the concert platform.

This is a widely-used Study, being quite easy but with just a little more work for the left-hand than some other studies used in the early stages of playing. The second half has nothing alarming in it, but it is in the first half where one or two tricky problems can arise. The first of these is caused by the 3rd finger which is needed on the low C in bar 2. If that was all that had to be done, there would be no trouble, but immediately before this we have to use the 4th finger for the D on the 2nd string, and this hinders the movement of the 3rd finger, so making life difficult. The way to tackle this is to position the 3rd finger over the 5th string 3rd fret, whilst playing the D with the 4th finger. Try this first without playing with the right hand, in other words silent practice. This will allow you to concentrate directly on the problems in the left hand. A similar thing is found in bar 4, this time in locating the top G, (4th finger). The cause of the trouble is once again our 3rd finger, and here the same system of practice will correct this — position the 4th finger over the top G on string one whilst playing bar 3. As in the last piece, do be careful not to leave bass notes ringing after their correct duration, e.g. the bass C in bar 3.

22 ANDANTINO BY CARCASSI

Here is another piece in C Major, also from the 19th century, written by another of the best-known guitarist/composers Matteo Carcassi, to whom we referred when discussing Carulli. Carcassi was born in Florence in 1792, and by the time he reached his teens he had made something of a reputation for himself as a player in his native Italy. However, it was not until he was twenty-eight that he decided to settle in Paris, then the artistic capital of the world. He had already toured in Germany where his performances were something of a sensation, and so Paris was the next logical step. In 1822 Carcassi came to England for the first time, and it seems he was equally as successful here and thereafter made annual visits to London. It was in the late 1820's that the French public's enthusiasm for Carulli's playing began to fade, and the new ideas of the younger and more virtuosic Carcassi, finally won the day. Carcassi toured extensively throughout most of his career, and it was only in the last few years of his life that he became reluctant to leave Paris. He died in 1853.

This short Andantino is a miniature written perhaps as a right hand study. Three new notes occur in it – a C sharp in the first complete bar of the second half, an F sharp in the next two bars and a bass G which appears in the third complete bar, and again just before the end of the work.

Example 16.

23 THE KEY OF G MAJOR

In an earlier chapter, we dealt with the construction of the major scale. We saw that it is always made up of the same pattern or arrangement of intervals, and that at the beginning of every piece – indeed, the start of each line of music – the composer puts the key signature. For C major, which was the key of our last two pieces, there are of course no sharps or flats, but in the next short piece we shall be tackling, because the key is G major, the key signature is written as follows;

Example 17.

To help you understand this a little better, play through the following scale:

Example 18.

It does not sound quite right. Listen carefully to the second note from the end, the F. To fit the pattern of intervals for the major scale, the last two notes should be only a semi-tone apart, and to achieve this we must sharpen or raise the F so that it now is played at fret 2.

Example 19.

In the two-octave version of the G major scale which appears below, the F sharp appears again, this time on the fourth string at fret 4. To save having to write in all these sharps, and to make the music clearer to read, the key-signature is used. In the case of G major this means that all F's at any pitch, are to be played sharp. Practise this scale in the same way as the scale of C Major, but when learnt, try variations of right hand fingering e.g. *i.a.* and *m.a.* The two new notes found in this scale are the following;

Scale of G major

Also

24 STUDY BY CARULLI

No major problems are encountered in this little Study in G major. However, before learning it, read once again the chapter on the rest stroke, for there are opportunities in the Study to use this technique. The type of rest-stroke would be the second one mentioned, where the finger tip perhaps collapses slightly, depending on the finger lengths and shapes of the individual. The idea is to bring out very slightly the melody notes in certain bars, playing with a full mellow tone quality. The notes in question have been marked with a V. Bars 1 and 5 in the second half should be read carefully, as the fingering is not absolutely straightforward, and one or two wrong notes could easily result. Remember, the numbers beside the notes indicate left-hand fingers, not frets.

The new note, C sharp, which appeared in the Andantino by Carcassi is also in this piece in bar nine. Notice though how it is cancelled out by the placing of a natural sign against the next note of C.

(In the type of writing found for example in bars 1 and 2, it is common practice to allow the quavers to ring on, rather than to try and cut them off. I have set out below the first bar as it should actually sound, and I think the rather cluttered appearance shows why it does not appear in print this way.)

Example 20.

Allegretto

F. Carulli

25 THE SCALE OF A MINOR

The major scale which has been mentioned already in this book, is a comparatively straightforward part of musical theory. To describe in simple and concise terms the *minor* scale is rather more difficult. Before doing this, let us look once again at the scale of C major.

Example 22.

We have here a set pattern for the intervals – *tone – tone – semitone – tone – tone – tone – semitone,* and the scale is always the same coming down as going up. One very important item to grasp before looking at the minor scale, is the function of the leading note which is immediately below the tonic or key note. In the case of the C Major scale, the leading note is B. The leading note does exactly what it says; it *leads* up to the tonic note when we go up the scale. Over many centuries, the ear has become accustomed to this interval of a semitone between the leading note and the tonic, (I refer now to music of the Western World), and this is also important to remember when we are dealing with minor scales.

In the minor scale, *the third note is always flattened* so that we begin tone – semitone. Rather than try and show how C major would be changed into C minor which is difficult because of the number of *flats* involved, it is easier to use the scale of A minor. Scales go in pairs, and every major scale has its own minor scale to accompany it. The musical term for this is the relative minor, in other words it is a relation of the Major scale. One other important point – they also share the same key signature. So, when there are no sharps or flats at the beginning of a piece, this tells us we are either in the key of C major, *or* A minor. How then do we know which key we are in? This is to do with the harmonic structure of the piece, and we shall be covering this in another chapter shortly.

For the moment, back to our scale of A minor. At the start of this scale we must have intervals of a tone and then a semitone, which gives the following:

Example 23.

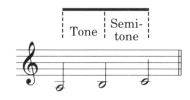

The next two notes are very easy, being D and E, in other words, the intervals of a tone and then another tone. We now have the first half of our scale:

Example 24.

The last part is the tricky part, because there are two possibilities open to us. There is the *harmonic* from of the minor scale which has as its three notes:

The only problem here is the awkward jump from F to G sharp, an interval of an augmented second, that is *three* semitones, which sounds a little strange to our ears. To avoid this, we use the other form of minor scale, the *melodic* which uses F sharp to smooth the way to the leading note (G sharp). Remember, from the leading note to the tonic should be a semitone, and therefore the leading note must be G sharp.

We can now complete our one-octave ascending A minor scale.

Example 25.

Having got up, there is the problem of coming down. The Melodic Minor Scale is slightly different descending. If we come down starting as follows:

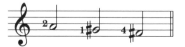

it sounds as though it is a Major scale we are playing. To give the effect of the minor scale, the first two notes are played a semitone lower, in this case G natural and F natural. Thereafter, the scale is the same;

Example 26.

We can now learn the complete one-octave scale of A minor, in its melodic form.

Scale of A minor

26 BASIC HARMONY

When we look at a piece of music, we are generally first attracted by the shape of the melody lines, in other words the tunes. These appear to be going along in a horizontal direction on the printed page. There is, however, another and equally important direction which music has, and that is vertical. In most music, if we take any one note of the main melody, underneath (or over the top) will be one or more notes which form the harmony. Even in single line pieces, e.g. parts of Bach's unaccompanied music for violin or 'cello, our mind is still putting in harmonies which at that particular point the solo instrument cannot play.

Why then should we know about harmony? It is essential we understand the structure of the music we are playing, and by so doing speak the same language as the composer, for each masterpiece, whether it be by Bach, Mozart, Beethoven Ravel, Bartók, has its own musical dialect, and unless we comprehend the basic laws of harmony it is impossible to really become deeply involved in what the composer is trying to say through his music. If we were to hear a basic chord of C major scored for orchestra by all the composers named earlier, each would have its own sound and colour, some using more woodwind, others perhaps more brass, some scoring the strings low down, etc. So when performing any piece, whether it be a large work such as a sonata or a concerto, or just a simple study of three lines, complete understanding of the musical structure is the most important thing. In music, the composer can very often convey a feeling impossible to express in words, by superb control and use of melody, harmony, and of course instrumentation.

Unfortunately, books on theory can be most confusing to the student who is in the earlier stages of learning an instrument, and what I propose to do here is simply to explain how a basic chord is made up. The simplest form is the **triad**. This is a group of three notes, made up of a **bass-note,** plus the **third** note above it, and also the **fifth** note above the bass. If C is taken as the bass-note, then the triad is made up with E and G.

Example 27.

Now because the **tonic** or key-note is forming the lowest note of the triad, it becomes the **root**, and the triad is then said to be in **root position.** Other variations on this basic triad would be, the point being, that they are all made up of the same three

elements, having C as their root. It does not always have to be a major chord, minor chords work in just the same way, e.g. A minor;

When one of the other notes of the basic triad is used as the bass-note, the chord is no longer in root position. To go back to C Major once again – if E is taken as the bass-note, the chord is then said to be in the **first inversion** (having the 3rd note up from the keynote as its bass). It would appear thus:

Example 28.

Finally, if the 5th note up from the tonic is used as the bass, the chord is said to be in its **second inversion.**

Example 29.

I hope this is not too confusing. I must repeat that this is the very basic theory of how chords (major and minor) are constructed, but I feel it is essential at this stage to have some idea of the way harmony works.

It is only comparatively recently that the lute has swept back to popularity thanks initially to the inspired playing of Julian Bream.

Lute music in England reached its peak at the time of Elizabeth I, and was probably the most popular instrument at the Royal Court during the 16th Century and throughout much of the 17th Century. Indeed, a lutenist was retained in the British court as late as the year 1752, when the instrument was rapidly becoming outdated and replaced by more modern instruments. Music for the lute was written in the form of *tablature*, which consisted of horizontal lines representing the strings, and letters or in some cases numbers, on or between these lines which indicated the particular fret to be depressed by a left-hand finger. The rhythm (or note values) was shown by special signs written above the notes (see figure 29).

Fig. 29 Robert Dowland, *A varietie of Lute Lessons* London, 1610

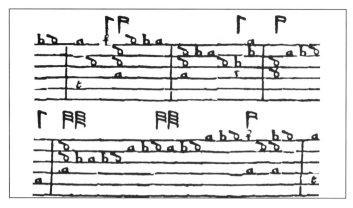

The little lute piece in this chapter comes from a famous collection of the Elizabethan era, known as the Jane Pickering Lute Book. The key is A minor, and there is only one new note to contend with, D sharp which will be found on string four, fret one.

Bars, 3, 4, and 6, all have awkward separation of the third and fourth fingers. In the 1st bar of the last section, A is fingered with three to allow the second finger to drop easily onto the bass B. Finally, in bar nine, there are the two big chords, the first of which contains our new note D sharp. This may look a handful of notes, but really this should present no major problem if the following procedure is carried out. Firstly, whilst playing the first chord, (B major, root position), have the third left-hand finger held about a quarter of an inch above the E on the fourth string, as this will help to get on to the second chord a little more smoothly. Also, always try to see which notes might be carried through into the chord which follows. Here the low B (fifth string) is one such case, and it makes sense to leave the middle finger pressing down on that note, while the rest of the hand locates the remainder of the chord which follows. This second chord, (E major, also root position), contains six notes, and obviously it is impossible to play all these together. Therefore, the chord must be spread or arpeggiated, in this instance using the right-hand thumb for all six strings, trying to take it as straight across the six as possible, which may mean arching the wrist a fraction just for this one chord. An angled thumb stroke will result in an unbalanced sound in the chord, with the top notes possibly sounding harsher than the bass. Another way of arpeggiating chords is to use a combination of thumb and fingers. In the case of a chord like this one of E major, the right-hand thumb would be used for the three bass strings, using rest-strokes for the first two notes to give a smooth transition from one string to the next. The three treble strings are then plucked with i.m.a., and, you may find it best to "place" these fingers on the strings at the commencement of the chord, "peeling" them off one by one smoothly and rapidly. The technical marking for an arpeggio is a wriggly line placed in front of the chord. One final point, the piece should sound unhurried, but flowing.

What if a day or a month or a year

From the Lute Book of
Jane Pickering

28 SLURS, ASCENDING AND DESCENDING

As has already been explained in an earlier chapter, when two or more notes of the same pitch are joined by a curved line, this indicates that the first note is played, and then held throughout the total value of the notes which follow. This tie line is not to be confused with a similar marking used to link two or more notes of *differing* pitch. In this latter instance, the notes concerned have to be *slurred,* played using just the left-hand fingers to produce the remaining notes once the first note has been sounded by the right hand. This will be more clearly seen in example 30.

Example 30.

There are two techniques for slurs, one for the ascending slur, and another for the descending. The ascending variety is produced by *hammering* down onto an already sounding string with a finger of the left hand. To understand this a little better, try the following exercise: pluck the open 1st string E, and then hammer down with the first finger of the left hand at fret one so producing the note F. The temptation is to rush the second note for fear that the plucked string will die away before you have had time to get the next note down. In fact, by making sure the finger hits absolutely square on the middle of the finger tip, that movement of this finger alone is used, and not by any turning of the hand, it will be possible, with practice, to produce a perfectly acceptable note by hammering down without even plucking the string first. The bad habit so easily acquired of using the rest of the hand to assist the finger, is in the end detrimental to technique. It is more likely when fingers two, three, and four are used, and slow concentrated practice should be directed towards strengthening these fingers so that they all work with equal power and accuracy.

This technical point also applies very much to the descending slur, where the second note is produced by pulling a left-hand finger down and across in the direction of the treble side of the fingerboard, in other words, in the direction of the palm of the hand. Now try this next exercise. Play C, first fret 2nd string, first finger of the left hand. Then by pulling the finger down towards the palm of the hand using the first and second joints only, try to produce a clear-sounding open B string. Next, try playing D (3rd fret on the same string, pressing down with the third finger). To produce the C, you must have the first finger in position on that note *before* pulling the third finger away from the D, this finger coming to rest momentarily against the 1st string (figures 30 & 31). There are several golden rules which must be followed in order to produce strong clear slurs. They are as follows:

1. Always press with the tips of the fingers.
2. Never use the hand or forearm to help slurs.
3. On descending slurs, make sure that the finger performing the slur moves only from joints 1 and 2.
4. In the case of a slur such as D to C (described above), one must counteract the pulling movement of the third finger at first by slightly pushing the *first* finger away from the hand. This will stop the string being pulled out of tune, or in the case of the first string stop it being pulled right off the edge of the finger-board!
5. Descending slurs on inside strings, (2 to 6), are generally a little more difficult, and the finger executing the slur should rest momentarily on the next string up in a kind of left-hand rest-stroke.
6. On ascending slurs if two fingers are involved, make sure the first of these remains down until the second has hammered down.
7. In descending slurs, in cases where two fingers are to be used such as D to C on the second string, the C should if at all possible, go down at the same time as the D.
8. Slurs should never be rushed. Always try and play them very strictly and rhythmically.

The following slur exercises should now be practised to thoroughly familiarize yourself with this technique.

Fig. 30

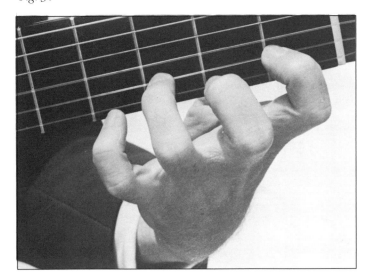

Fig. 31

Exercise 14.

Exercise 15.

Exercise 16.

There are many other possible slur exercises, indeed the ingenious student can work out his or her own studies, but a cautionary word must be introduced here – if at any time the pupil experiences any muscular pain whilst practising, they should stop immediately as to continue would mean risking serious and perhaps permanent damage to the hand. This is particularly so with the practice of slurs, and barrés which will be introduced shortly. To conclude this chapter, here are a few more slur exercises. Because the student has still to learn many of the notes in the lower part of the fingerboard, to save confusion, these exercises have been written out stating simply the string number, and which finger is to be used. *For the purposes of these studies, the student may take it that these fingering indications also mean the fret numbers.* However, once each separate exercise has been learnt, the finger pattern dealt with therein may be transferred progressively up the fingerboard, one position or fret at a time.

These are to be played commencing on string 1, continuing without a break across strings 2 3 4 5 6, and then back again. When string 1 is reached, start on the next pattern. For a variation on this, as mentioned in the previous paragraph, each pattern may be played going up or down the same string rather than across the other strings. The idea is always to try and vary your practice, as exact repetition leads to boredom and staleness.

(3 times for each pattern)

122334	433221	121314	413121	142434	434241
132432	143231	134232	213243	342312	314214

29 SCALE OF A MINOR (2ND OCTAVE) AND A STUDY BY MERTZ

Before tackling this next piece by Mertz, it is necessary to deal with several points. The piece is in A minor, and it uses a number of notes still to be learnt. Firstly, it will be of considerable help to get to know the two-octave form of the A minor scale, as this will cover a couple of these notes, and also properly introduce you to shifts, or position changes in the left hand. The second octave is as follows:

Example 31.

Remember that as it is the **melodic** form of the minor scale, the scale changes slightly on the way back down. So to begin with middle A, the top note of the scale as learnt so far, it is plain sailing most of the way. A is followed by open B, then C and D, first and third frets, second string. Next is open E, and after this things become a little tougher. Our next note is F sharp, second fret, **but first finger,** in other words, we now have to move the whole hand up one fret, keeping the thumb in contact with the neck of the instrument at the same time, so that we now play at position two, this being the fret at which the first finger is playing. After F sharp comes G sharp, fret four but third finger. Remember not to let the left-hand position change, still press with the tips of the fingers, and all four fingers bent nicely (figure 32). To complete the ascending part of this scale, there is just A, fifth fret, fourth finger. I suggest learning this part thoroughly before going on the descending part of the scale, as there is quite a bit to think about.

Fig. 32

Coming down from the A, the next note is G natural, third fret, but depressed with the fourth finger. Now this movement off the A and down onto the G is most important. It must sound absolutely smooth, with no break between the notes, and to achieve this we must slide the fourth finger down without losing contact with the string. A simple sliding motion will sound sloppy, as the G sharp between the two notes will be heard, so this will not do. The correct way to make the change smooth and at the same time clean and clear, is to take the pressure off the A, keeping in contact with the string, and then slide down very, very quickly, putting back the pressure when the G is reached. In downward shifts like this the thumb usually lifts away from the back of the guitar neck momentarily, but at the same time not allowing the fingers to drift out of position. The thumb goes back on immediately the shift has been performed. I personally find it impossible to maintain contact with the thumb in downward shifts. To begin with one is working against gravity, and also there is a tendency for the thumb to stick or judder if kept in contact.

The remainder of the scale is straightforward, the only new note being F natural, which has already been learnt.

A few more notes must still be covered before going onto the piece. On the 6th string up to now only G (3rd fret) has been used. F sharp appears in the new piece, and will be found at fret two, and while we are there, we may as well cover F (natural) which is at fret one, even though it is not used in the Mertz Study.

Example 32.

Towards the end of the piece, a very high note suddenly appears. This is top E and is not as bad as it looks, in fact it is quite easy to find and remember, for it comes on the first string at fret twelve, (where the neck and the body of the guitar meet). This note is an octave above the open string.

Example 33.

At the beginning of the very last bar, we have A (top note of the scale), and underneath a C which normally would be played on the second string. This however makes a difficult stretch, and instead we take this note on the third string at fret five, so missing out the second string altogether.

Example 34.

Over certain notes in the Study will be seen curious signs which resemble a letter V on its side, e.g.

These are an indication that the note is to be played with greater *attack* than its neighbours. This marking should not be confused with the sign: ⫟ indicating a slight accent and sustaining effect. There is a subtle difference, the first being the more dramatic of the two. To achieve this attack, it is necessary to use a right-hand rest-stroke for the note in question. Slow practise is suggested perhaps just on the first bar to begin with, until your hand has become used to this mixing up of free and rest-strokes. Also, watch out for the several left-hand slurs which occur throughout the piece. They are all the same in fact, being from F to E on the first string.

The D sharp (in bar twelve) was learnt in the lute piece What if a Day, but please do not overlook the fact that it becomes D natural later in the bar. Finally, watch out for the new note on the sixth string F sharp, normally it would be fingered with second finger, but here to make the change to the next bass note easier, it has been fingered with the third.

Johann Kaspar Mertz is another of the most famous 19th Century guitarist-composers, being born in 1806 at Pressburg, Hungary, and dying in Vienna in 1856. His parents although extremely poor, encouraged him during his early years in the study of music, Mertz being self-taught on both the guitar and flute. By the age of 12, he had decided to concentrate almost completely on the guitar, but it was not until the age of 34 that he started to gain recognition due to his moving to Vienna in the year 1840. His breakthrough came in November that year when he performed as soloist at the Court Theatre under the patronage

of the Empress Carolian Augusta, for whom he later became court guitarist. Concerts followed in Cracow and Warsaw, Berlin, Dresden, and Leipzig. In 1842, Mertz married concert pianist Miss Josephine Plantin, and a year later they settled in Vienna. Unfortunately, their marriage was to be a comparatively short one, for Mertz's health, never good, became steadily worse from about 1846 onwards. The number of his recitals became less each year, and the strain of touring, plus illnesses mild and severe gradually took their toll. The effect of the winter of 1855/1856 was the final blow from which he never fully recovered, and he died on 14th October 1856.

Mertz was a celebrated composer of guitar music during his lifetime, but in the 20th Century it is the names of Carulli, Sor, Giuliani, we are inclined to remember. Nevertheless, Mertz wrote a vast number of works, not only for solo guitar, but also incorporating guitar with other instruments. Two interesting facts are worth mentioning here in connection with Mertz. He was very exact about right-hand fingering in his pieces, and the need for using alternate fingers. Also, we tend these days to think of the ten-string guitar as played by people like Narciso Yepes as being a recent development. However we learn that Mertz had already considered the possibilities of this, and used one for many of his recitals!

The marking at the beginning of the piece is *allegro*, which means fairly fast, or lively. This is only a finished tempo, for practise purposes, play at half or even a quarter of what you consider to be your ultimate speed.

Study in A minor

J.K. Mertz

30 SCALE OF E MINOR

The key-signature of E minor is  which it shares with the key of G major. A quick way to find the relative minor of any Major key is simply to count down two notes from the tonic note of the Major scale. In this case with G being the Major key, two steps below this is E = E minor. The actual interval is a tone and a half, so that in the case of A Major, the relative minor is F sharp.

In this new scale of E minor (two octaves), all F's are of course sharp, and in addition, all C's and D's are sharpened going up the scale, and are played as naturals coming back down.

The only note to be careful of is the low C sharp which might catch you out, this is at the fourth fret on the fifth string.

Scale of E minor.

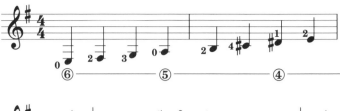

31 WALTZ IN E MINOR — CARULLI

This is a very well-known piece by Ferdinando Carulli, being in reality a study for the right hand *m* and *a* fingers, which as you will see are used alternately for most of the first half. This first half is not difficult as far as the left hand is concerned, and there is indeed only one place which needs explanation in the second half where the piece moves into the related Major key, G Major. In bar two of this second half, (bar 18 of the whole piece), we must play the D with first finger, so that the left hand is then at **position three**. The aim is to let the top notes continue sounding and so the next note (B) cannot be played as an open string, but must be taken on string three, fret four, and depressed with the second finger. This shift to the third position should be practised in the same way as the slide in the A minor scale, that is releasing the pressure on the left-hand fingers, but *not* losing contact with

Fig. 33

the strings, also not forgetting that we must slide the second finger also from A to B on the third string.

One very interesting point which you may have noticed in the lute piece What if a Day, is that in certain chords the left hand cannot always be held in the single-note position of being parallel to the edge of the fingerboard. Bars 3 and 4 of the Waltz are good examples, where the hand must be turned, pivoting on the thumb, and by moving the whole arm, enabling each of the fingers to come up close to the fret (figure 33).

Two more points: the time signature is $\frac{3}{8}$, that is, three *eighth* notes per bar. Keep the tempo steady and do not rush. At the end there is printed D.C. *al Fine*. This means go back to the beginning of the piece and repeat up to the word *Fine*. (D.C. stands for *da capo* – repeat from the beginning.) *Fine* means the end or finish of the piece.

Finally, this may be a good time to list the main indication for tempo found at the beginning of pieces or sections. Most of them have already been mentioned, but a table of these markings will be found quite useful to refer back to.

Largo	Slow and dignified
Larghetto	Similar to Largo, but a little faster
Adagio	Slowly, though not as slow as Largo or Larghetto
Andante	Slowish but at the same time flowing
Andantino	Slightly slower or faster than Andante, depending on the individual composer
Allegretto	Quite lively
Allegro	Fairly fast – lively
Presto	Quick
Prestissimo	Very quick

(In a piece such as this, where a D.C. is indicated, it is normal to not observe any repeat signs the *last* time through that particular section, up to the *FINE* indication.)

Waltz

Ferdinando Carulli

32 THE HALF BARRÉ

A *barré* is a technique whereby a finger of the left hand, usually the first finger, is used to stop more than one string. As the strings on a classical guitar are quite widely separated, all but the largest of finger-tips will not press down more than one string, and so the finger has to be laid flat across the fingerboard behind any given fret, so that two, three or more strings can be depressed.

With the half-barré, it is usual to press three strings, that is to say *any three adjacent strings*, be they 1 2 & 3, or 3 4 & 5 etc. It is much easier to think of a half-barré in this way, indeed the technical aspect is much safer, than to always be in doubt as to whether to cover two or three strings, even though the third string under the half-barré may not be used.

Fig. 34

The correct technique is to bend the first finger normally at the second joint, but then to collapse the first joint slightly, and then press a little on the outside of the finger, (see figure 34). If you try to press straight down, the left-hand position becomes awkward and unnatural. The best way to practise this is away from the guitar. Just try collapsing the finger directly against your left thumb, to loosen up the first joint (figure 35).

There are three main reasons why we do the half-barré this way. Firstly, by collapsing, it is possible to get tremendous pressure, so reducing the risk of buzzes and rattles. Secondly, the other fingers are not pushed out of position. Thirdly, in the case of a barré covering strings 2 3 and 4, the open 1st string can often be left free to vibrate.

At first, it may be difficult to collapse the first finger, while holding the other fingers normally. An exercise which will help in this problem is the following. This is for the left hand alone. Press down the first string at frets six, seven, and eight, with the 2nd, 3rd, and 4th fingers respectively. Ensure these fingers are correctly positioned, and that you are pressing with the tips. Now slowly place the 1st finger on string *three* at fret five. Finally, collapse the first finger, so ending up with a half-barré across strings 1, 2, and 3. The other fingers should still be held on the first string. When you feel happy about doing this, try reversing the process. This is excellent practice before taking on the real thing in the next piece. The sign for a barré is C, (from the

Fig. 35

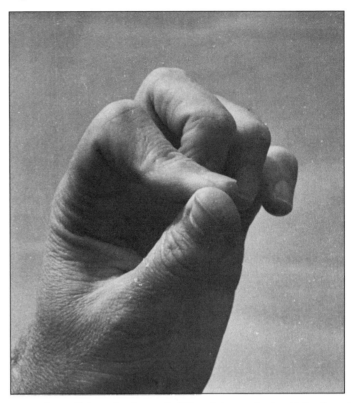

Spanish *cejilla*), and when a half-barré is required a ½ is placed in front.

Menuet — Kuhnau

It is very nice to be able to present this piece here, because not only is it a little Gem, but it also has several very interesting things in it, which make it all the more worthwhile to study. Johann Kuhnau was born in Geising, Saxony in 1660 and died in Leipzig in 1722. His music I think deserves to be heard a lot more than it actually is, for he was an important composer, indeed Bach's predecessor as Cantor of the Thomas School in Leipzig, and a composer for clavichord and harpsichord of a very high order. He was one of the earliest composers to compose Sonatas rather than Suites, and his works contain much 'programme music', that is music which interprets a story of some kind. This Menuet has a great deal of imitative writing, and the student should analyse each bar very carefully as the piece will then make a lot more sense. The opening is in the style of a *canon*, where the first phrase is repeated by the lower part before the it has been completed resulting in an overlapping effect – indeed this device is used many times in the piece and is most effective. The other interesting thing this piece introduces is the *hemiola* which is a rhythmic device used to change the position of the main accents in a bar, or in this case over a two-bar section so as to make these two bars sound like one longer bar. The places in the Menuet where this happens are in bars 14 and 15 and 22 and 23. Each bar has 3 quarter-notes as its value, but because in these particular bars we need to accent *every other*

Bars 14 & 15

Bars 22 & 23

beat, we are really doing away mentally with the bar line in the middle, and making one long bar of *three half-notes*. If you are still confused, I have written these bars out again here as we have to interpret them.

By the way, two little bits of fingering I must mention. In bar 15, the B in the opening chord has to be played on fret 4, 3rd string, and not as an open string, because the note must be held on for the whole beat, which is impossible if played as an open B, as it would then be cut off when you put down the D following the chord. Also, in the 5th bar from the end of the piece, the bass D is fingered on the 5th string, fret 5, as it is absolutely impossible to play it as an open string. Don't forget, the note above it is F *sharp*, (fret 4). The following note (G) could be played as an open string, but here I choose for the sake of clarity of sound to play it on string 4, fret 5.

In my recording of this piece I have incorporated several ornaments which is the correct interpretation for music of this period. These are executed by means of left-hand slurs, beginning on the note above the written note and played rapidly

Menuet

J. Kuhnau

33 ALLEGRETTO BY GIULIANI

Mauro Giuliani is regarded by many present-day guitar aficionados, as the best of the nineteenth-century guitarists. There seems to be some doubt as to the exact year of his birth, but 1781 is now thought to be correct. There are in fact similarities with the career of Mertz, for Giuliani did not really achieve any sort of recognition until he moved from his native Italy to Vienna in 1806. His superb playing soon brought fame, and very favourable reports in the press, indeed it is certain that Beethoven attended one of his recitals, and also possibly Schubert. Giuliani was one of a group of musical celebrities who established an orchestra primarily for performances of Beethoven's music. In 1819, Giuliani was forced to leave Vienna in rather curious circumstances, having it seems had charges brought against him. He went to Venice, and then Rome, finally moving on to Naples where in 1826 he played before Francis 1. However, Giuliani's health was already beginning to fail, and three years later on 8th May, he died.

His death, at such a comparatively young age, was a tragic loss to the guitar. Apart from being a performer of the highest calibre, his compositions are equalled in the 19th century only by those of the great Fernando Sor. Giuliani's works are frequently heard in recitals today, included in these are the famous Sonata Op. 15, the Sonatinas Op. 71, and the beautiful Variations on Handel's Harmonious Black-smith. He also wrote several guitar concertos, of which the Concerto in A Major for guitar and strings is now the most popular. His compositions are extremely melodic, superbly conceived for the instrument, and very rich in harmonies. His studies, particularly the more advanced ones, are of a very high standard indeed, and are ideal material for the would-be concert performer. It is perhaps sad that these studies have been overshadowed to some extent by the celebrated studies of Fernando Sor, and consequently somewhat neglected.

The Allegretto comes from Giuliani's book of easy pieces entitled The Butterfly. The time signature is $\frac{6}{8}$, six beats in the bar, each beat being worth an eighth note. Several points which are worth taking out and studying separately are the following: the double slur in the first complete bar. Here we are in position two and must hammer down the third finger onto B (4th fret) and then fourth finger onto C (5th fret). These grace-notes, and the one in bar 18 should be played quickly and lightly. Bars 12 and 13 are worth close study. There is a fingering pattern here with the E played on the second string at fret five. The G sharp and the F sharp although only written as eighth notes should be held on over the top of the E and the D respectively. In the second bar from the end, we have our first half-barré. If you have practised the exercise in the previous chapter, this barré will present absolutely no problems, coming as it does on strings 1, 2, and 3, at fret five. Half way through bar four, there is a tricky bit of fingering. Please note that the 3rd finger is carried down from the C to the B, and that the second finger has to depress the sixteenth note F, because the first finger is needed for the middle G sharp. Only one new note appears in this piece – low G sharp, which is on string six, fret 4.

Example 35.

⑥ (Fret 4)

Finally, in this piece we encounter dotted rhythm for the first time. To play this correctly, try it slowly, counting the three beats, but not actually playing anything on beat two. A dot after a note lengthens it by half its value, so the second note in the group falls in between beats two and three; e.g.

Allegretto

Mauro Giuliani

34 SCALE OF D MAJOR & LADY LAITON'S ALMAIN BY DOWLAND

This is just a one-octave scale which will introduce you to the piece by John Dowland. The key-signature is *two* sharps, so as well as all F's being sharp, the same will now apply to all C's. Notice that the scale is fingered in the second position, that is, first finger pressing at the 2nd fret.

Now on to the piece. John Dowland was born near Dublin in 1562 and was the finest lutenist of his day. Most of his life however was spent further afield, and on three separate occasions he held the position of court lutenist to the King of Denmark. Although all his printed music was first issued in England, many works were subsequently published in such places as Paris, Antwerp, Cologne, Leipzig, Hamburg, and Amsterdam. He wrote some of the finest lute pieces of all time, pavanes, galliards, and the more extended fantasies, but he is remembered mainly for his many songs with lute accompaniment. The earliest of these appeared in 1597, and was entitled *First Booke of Songes or Ayres . . . with Tableture for the Lute.* Such was its popularity, it went through four editions in the

composer's lifetime! What made these songs great was the expressiveness of the melodies, the sensitive appreciation of the words, plus the inspired use of the lute for the accompaniments. Like many composers, Dowland seems to have been somewhat neglected towards the end of his life, and he died poor and embittered in London in 1626.

Lady Laiton's Almain is one of the easier examples of this great composer's work, but it is still a very attractive piece. The time-signature is Alla breve, that is Common time but with a vertical line through it which turns it into 2 beats in the bar, rather than 4. Bar three is worth separate study as the left-hand fingering is a little cumbersome. In bar eleven, the last note E is played on the second string (fret five) to balance the tone with the D's on either side, and also to do away with an open E which would continue sounding throughout the next bar. This happens again in the sixth and second bars from the end of the piece. This time, the E's are the second of two 16th notes, and are slurred.

Lady Laiton's Almain

John Dowland

35 TONE COLOUR ON THE GUITAR

Fig. 36

For a large part of the time the right hand plays just below the soundhole, (figure 36). This is where the standard range of sounds on the guitar are produced. However, varying degrees of colour may be obtained by a simple movement of the hand in either direction along the strings. For example, a harsh or metallic sound is produced by moving the hand towards the bridge. How close to the bridge will depend upon the character of the instrument, and also how brittle you wish the sound to be, but a rough distance would be about 30 mm (1½ inches) to where the middle or third fingers are plucking.

To allow the hand to play comfortably nearer the bridge, a slight adjustment in the position of the forearm on the edge of the guitar is required. It is necessary to rest further from the elbow, maybe as much as an inch, if the wrist is to remain at the correct height (figure 37). The technical term for this colour is *ponticello,* or as it usually appears in music, ponti. There is a good opportunity of trying this out in a short section of the Lady Laiton's Almain by Dowland. This passage commences with the last note of bar four, and continues through to the end of bar eight.

Fig. 36

In addition to plucking below the soundhole, it is sometimes a nice effect to play right over the soundhole – or even over the 19th fret. This colour I have always called *dolce* (sweet), and it is quite well suited to passages in lute pieces, as it is a little like the soft, warm sound of that particular instrument. Once again, the Dowland is a good place to try this tone colour, in the section between bars 13 and 16, (except the very last note, which is the beginning of a new phrase and therefore must have a different tone).

Just as the right arm had to be adjusted with the ponticello effect, so when the hand moves up over the soundhole the arm should go with it, which means resting a fraction *nearer* the elbow.

The guitar is a marvellous instrument because it is capable of such rich textures and tone colour, but changes in tone can easily become vulgar if they are done in a random fashion. Always consider the type of piece you are playing, the period in which it was written, and then if it needs tone colour variations, just how much would be considered in good taste.

36 MORE ABOUT SCALES

I would like now to take a little bit of space to go over what we have learnt so far about scales. Five scales have been covered, C Major, A minor, G major, E minor, and D major. We have seen what makes up a scale, the set pattern for the major form, plus the two types of minor scale which share the same key signature. The relative minor scale can be worked out by counting two notes down from the major scale's tonic note. So we found that the relative minor of C major is A minor, and so on. It will be noticed that only sharp keys have been dealt with up to now. Most guitar pieces are in sharp keys, anything up to four sharps in the key signature is quite common. This is simply because all the open strings of the guitar are tuned to the tonic notes of sharp keys, E major (four sharps), B major (five sharps), G major (one sharp), D major (two sharps), and A major (three sharps). Flat keys on the guitar generally do not lie very well, and it is quite rare to find a piece written in four flats. One flat (F major) is encountered quite often however, and we shall be dealing with this shortly.

There are a couple of useful points to remember if you have difficulty learning key signatures. These only apply to sharp keys however. Assuming we know that a key signature without sharps or flats is C major, the sharp keys then go up a fifth for each sharp added to the key signature. Five notes up from C is G. (G major has one sharp.) Five up from G is D. (Two sharps), etc. Another system comes into effect if we are confronted by a key signature in sharps which is unfamiliar to us. In this case, always take the last sharp of the key signature, and raise it a semitone. This will give the key, or at least the Major key (the harmony will then tell you if it is in the relative minor). So let's see if this works. Supposing we were given a piece in the following key:

The last sharp is D sharp, and a semitone up from this gives us the key of E major.

In this book I only intend going up to two sharps. This will enable the student to tackle a vast number of pieces, and to let his technique settle down, without being confronted with difficult key-signatures. However, as I mentioned earlier, the key-signature of one flat occurs quite regularly, and so this must be learnt, the keys being F major, and its relative D minor.

37 SCALE OF F MAJOR

Before going through the full two-octave version of this scale, the student may care to work out the basic single-octave scale, starting on the fourth string, fret three. One note must be flattened, the question is which one?

Example 36.

Remember the interval pattern for the major scale: tone – tone – semitone – tone – tone – tone – semitone. There should be just a semitone between A and B and so the B must be flattened bringing it down to the third fret. The scale then continues normally with C, D, E, and F.

Example 37.

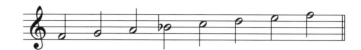

Now try the two-octave form. The other B flat is on string five, fret *one*.

By the way, do not forget to practise *all* your scales in two's and four's as with C major.

Scale of F major

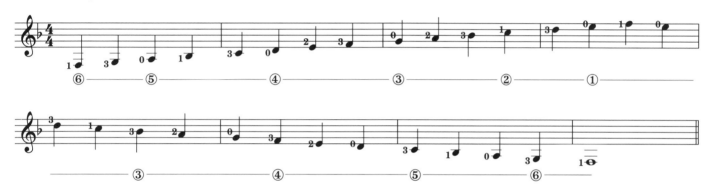

38 THE FULL BARRÉ

Fig. 38

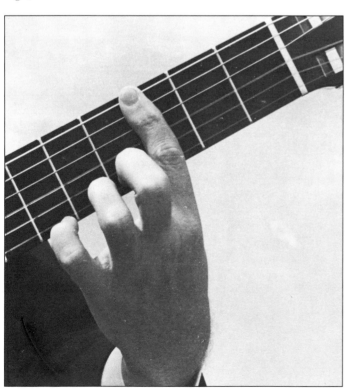

Before tackling a piece in the new key of F major, it will be necessary to cover just one more technical hurdle. This is the **FULL BARRÉ** where the first finger of the left hand presses down all six strings at a given fret. It is far simpler to train the finger into depressing six strings, the instances of barrés where only four or five strings must be covered being comparatively rare. To begin with , great strength will be needed to do this, and I would suggest practising full barrés at frets three, four, and five, where they are a little easier. Try the following method: press down the first finger across all six strings at the third fret, keeping the finger dead straight, the wrist is needed but not too much, (figure 38). Aim to get the finger as close to the fret as possible without deadening any of the notes. Once you feel you have the barré safely covering the six strings, play each one with the thumb, beginning with the sixth string to check for any rattles, etc. The third string is usually the trouble spot as it tends to lie in the second joint of the barré finger. After a time it is possible to direct more pressure towards that part of the barré, or if this fails, to simply move the finger a fraction further across so that the finger-tip projects *slightly* over the edge of the fingerboard. As with the half barré, the finger naturally rests slightly on its side (figure 39).

Fig. 39

This is by far the most difficult technique learnt so far, and it cannot be stressed strongly enough, that as soon as any pain occurs when practising full barrés, stop immediately, and let the hand recover, otherwise permanent damage can result. The hand will naturally strengthen in its own good time. When you are reasonably happy with your full-barré, try the short prelude by Carcassi. The half-barré in bar five covers strings two, three, and four, and there is a guide finger in bars six and seven when the second finger remains on the third string, moving from A to B flat, and back to A again.

Prelude

Carcassi

39 STUDY BY FERNANDO SOR

The greatest guitarist of the 19th Century, Fernando Sor was born in Barcelona on 13th February 1778. His father being a good amateur guitarist, the young Fernando naturally was attracted to the instrument. Sor was educated at the monastery in Montserrat, where he gained his knowledge of harmony and composition. Upon leaving the monastery at the age of seventeen, Sor returned to Barcelona where he continued his study of the guitar. Two years later saw him based in Madrid under the patronage of the Duchess of Alba. Unfortunately, due to the death of the Duchess in 1802, Sor was left without support, but was then taken into the protection of the Duke of Medina-Celi, a period which was to last for several years until political unrest prompted Sor to move to Paris. Shortly after this he visited London giving a number of hugely successful recitals. Returning to Paris for the production of his ballet *Cendrillon,* Sor met with such public acclaim, and financial success that he was now able to continue his travels on a much wider basis as a recitalist, one of the countries he visited being Russia, where he performed in Moscow and St. Petersburg. The final part of his life was spent, apart from one short trip to England, in Paris, where he died in 1839 leaving behind a vast number of com-

positions for guitar, many of which are standard items in recitals today. Among these are the set of Variations on a theme of Mozart, several sonatas, fantasias, minuets, and a large number of very fine studies.

The Larghetto in A minor is one of Sor's best-known pieces in the easier technical category. Please observe the position three indications in bars one, three, and four, and also the half-barré in bar five. The second half begins with the two full-barrés, at frets three, and one. A single play through should show you that there is a fingering pattern here, and this is the best way to remember this passage. In bar seven, second half, we have a curious little extra note on the first beat. This is an *acciaccatura,* a very short note played with the two A's which make up the rest of the chord, but then slurred extremely quickly producing the C. The effect is of the C to still sound as though it comes on the first beat of the bar, but with a very quick *grace* note crushed in ahead of it. Sometimes more than one note is used, an example of which appears six bars from the end. Here we have to get in three notes, a *triple appogiatura,* before the main note on the beat. This means hammering down F followed by G, and then pulling off the G to give the quarter-note F.

Larghetto

Fernando Sor

40 PRELUDE NO.4 — MOLINO

Francesco Molino, or as he later became known, Don Francois Molino, was one of the most travelled of the better-known late 18th and early 19th Century guitarists/composers. Born in Florence in 1775 he learnt the violin and guitar at a fairly early age, and made such good progress that several friends by their generosity enabled him to devote himself to the field of music. Molino later studied in Turin, eventually becoming musical theatrical director there. From Turin, he decided to move on to other centres in Italy, and then to Germany. By the year 1820, he was in Paris where his performances on both violin and guitar found great praise, and he decided to spend several months in that city. Next stop was Spain where he played before the Court of Madrid. It was whilst in Spain that the Spanish prefix to his

Prelude No.4

F. Molino

name was acquired. His stay in Spain lasted a number of years, after which he spent some time in London, and then moved back to Paris, dying there in 1847. Prelude No.4 is I feel, a good piece for study in that it includes some extended arpeggio playing, slurs, and a little barré work. A very important detail found in bars 1, 3, and 5, is the observance of the rests. As soon as the 2nd bass note is played the chord should be stopped by placing the thumb and fingers back on the strings. In bar 6, there is a slur from B to A, 3rd to 1st fingers, and here the hand must not be turned outwards during the slur, just use the action of the 3rd finger alone to execute the slur. If incorrectly done, the 4th finger will be carried away from the 2nd string, so making it difficult to hit the next note, G, fret eight string two. Notice too how the right-hand fingering changes slightly in the arpeggio figure, e.g. between that in bar 9, and the one found in bar 13. In this second pattern the thumb moves across from string 5 to string 4 each time, so bringing the fingers into position to play the other strings. There are several opportunities to make use of guide fingers, e.g. in bars 7 to 8; 15 to 16 (4th finger moving from C sharp to D sharp). New notes are G on string two, fret 8, and A sharp, string five, fret 1.

41 TWO-OCTAVE SCALE OF C MAJOR

Seeing we have just dealt with the high B and C on the first string, this is a good time to cover the two-octave C Major Scale.

All the notes have been mentioned already in this book, so it is simply a matter of going through the left-hand fingering, to check on any possible problems. The second octave in fact starts easily enough, going from middle C on the second string. The next four notes D, E, F, and G are all straightforward, and it is only with the top three notes that we encounter any problem. Left-hand shifts have already been discussed, and so with the note A the hand should move up to the fifth position, so that the first finger drops onto that note, having been used as a guide from the F. Remember to release the pressure on the F after the G has been sounded for its full value. The first finger then slides up the string to A on the fifth fret, maintaining contact all the time. The left thumb should also be in contact with the back of the neck as it slides up with and slightly in advance of the first finger. During this shift, do not let the other fingers move away from their normal positions hovering over the strings. The B and C can now be played using third and fourth fingers on frets seven and eight.

Coming back down the scale, after the A the left hand returns to the first position. In this shift once again use the first finger as the guide keeping it in contact with the string but without sufficient pressure to make contact with the frets. The first finger slides down from A to F whilst the third finger is kept back for the G. As soon as the first finger reaches F, apply pressure and also drop the third finger onto G. Don't forget that the thumb follows immediately behind the first finger during the shift, coming off the back of the neck for a split second, but going on again as soon as the F is reached. The rest of the scale should present no difficulties.

Scale of C major (2 octaves)

42 A FEW MORE REMARKS ABOUT BASIC HARMONY

In an earlier chapter we learnt about how basic triads are made up, and their inversions. Also, how the keynote of a scale is called the *tonic*, and how the note immediately below this is called the *leading* note.

There are just five other notes in the scale to cover, and these are as follows:

2nd . . . . *Supertonic*

3rd . . . . *Mediant*

4th . . . . *Sub-dominant*

5th . . . . *Dominant*

6th . . . . *Sub-mediant*

This last one, the sub-mediant, is of course the note on which the relative minor scale begins.

In music, to create interest, variety, atmosphere, colour, whatever you like to call it, the composer is constantly changing the underlying harmony, or chordal structure. We know that a chord of C major has to consist of three ingredients, the *tonic* note, the 3rd note of the scale which is the *mediant*, and the 5th note which is the *dominant:*

Now, if we were to go on playing this chord all day and night it might become a little boring – so we change to another chord, the most common one being a chord of the *dominant,* in other words, a chord which is based upon the *5th note of the home key.* The dominant note in the key of C is G, and a triad based upon this note would contain G, and the third and fifth notes above it, namely B and D.

Example 41.

So we say the piece moves from *tonic* to *dominant,* or in popular jargon, one to five. To add variety to this, we can have a sequence of chords which go *Tonic; Sub-mediant; Sub-dominant; Dominant; Tonic;* that is triads based on 1, 6, 4, 5, and 1 degrees of the scale. In C major this would give the following:

Example 42.

The fun starts when other notes are added to triads, the most common of these is the seventh added to the Dominant triad. Seven notes up from G (Dominant of C major), is F natural, and if this is added to the dominant triad we get what is called a chord of the dominant 7th.

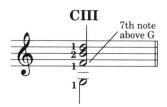

Example 43.

If you play this chord, you will notice it has an uneasy feel to it – it is not complete in some way, and this is because the new note F is wanting to move down to E, and the whole chord needs to what is called *resolve.* The most straightforward resolution would be back to the *tonic* chord of C major.

Example 44.

When you are practising your pieces, in future try to analyse what is happening in the harmony. It will really help you learn much more easily, and give you a better understanding of what the composer is saying in the piece.

43 LESSON IN A MINOR BY SOR

This is another very popular study-piece by Fernando Sor. The two high notes B and C have been covered in the two-octave scale of C major (Chapter 41) and should cause no problem. Do check very carefully the left-hand fingering in bars one and two, as it moves from the fifth position to the fourth. The last note of bar three (A), is fingered with one to allow a smoother change to the next chord. The shift between bars five and six should be practised thoroughly. When moving down from the A (5th fret, first string), keep the finger in contact with the string so that the first finger comes to rest *on* the F at the same time as you play the G (4th finger.) Four bars from the end there is a big jump up from first to fifth position. The secret here is to

not let the fourth finger waggle about, but keep it hovering over the first string as you play the first chord, *and* as you move the hand up the fingerboard afterwards. Direct your eyes on the note you are aiming at, the top C (fret eight), concentrate, and all will be well. The third bass note of that same bar for ease of fingering is best taken on the sixth string at fret seven. To make the shift smooth in the treble line from B down to A, keep the *third* finger in contact with the string, sliding it down to the fourth fret at the same time placing the fourth finger on the A (5th fret). If this proves really impossible, the 3rd finger can be used for the A and G which follow.

Study

Capriccio — Giuliani

This is certainly one of the most widely taught pieces by Giuliani, and is a fine technical study for both hands, as well as being a very good sounding work. The construction is excellent, with imitative writing in treble and bass, e.g. bar 1, I feel it is a mistake to strike the D sharp with the thumb the C, B & A, yes certainly as it is these notes which are imitated in the bass line at the end of the bar. (The same thing applies in bar 3.) At bar 11 you will notice a nasty jump between the 8th and 9th notes. This is because the 1st finger has to move directly from the A to the F, (3rd string to 1st string). If we follow the music closely, the bass C sharp should be held until the 8th note has been played. However, an alternative fingering would be to let the C sharp bass go after the 6th note of the bar sliding down with the 4th

finger from A to G, and fingering the next note (A) with 2. The following F can then be arrived at smoothly. So the alternative fingering would appear in print as follows:

The four-bar section which begins at bar 16 has three technical points to observe.

1. The movement across the strings by the right hand in the first half of the bar.
2. The jump to a higher position midway through the bar.
3. The left-hand slurs. With the second of these problems, your task will be made easier if, when you change position, the 1st and 4th fingers are held over the 1st string, ready to drop down onto their respective notes, the position change actually being made whilst the 7th and 8th notes of the bar are being played.

Capriccio

Giuliani

Allegro

44 THE MUSIC OF GASPAR SANZ

In this book we have mentioned and included pieces by many celebrated guitarists, but no collection would be complete without the music of Gaspar Sanz, the leading player in Spain during the 17th Century.

Sanz was born in Salamanca in 1640, and received his education at the University, where he gained the degree of Bachelor of Theology, and later became a Professor of Music. His famous book of instruction for guitar appeared in 1674, and constitutes Sanz's total output for the instrument. His compositions are in direct contrast with Spanish music a century before, and indeed French 17th century guitar music, both of which very much reflect the elegance and atmosphere of the Royal court. The music of Sanz is taken from the market-place and the theatre – dances and songs, popular at the time. Many and varied are the titles of his pieces; Danza de las Hachas, Canarios, La Caballeria de Napoles, Españoleta, etc., and today a high percentage of guitar recitals feature the work of this important composer.

I have grouped together a set of Three Short Pieces; Paradetas, Españoleta, and Matachin, to represent Gaspar Sanz in this tutor. *Paradetas* is interesting, because the whole piece is played at second position. There is nothing technically difficult about it except perhaps the embellishments in bars two and fifteen. These *mordents* are somewhat like the grace notes in the Larghetto by Sor. The first note of the mordent comes *on* the beat, the left hand executing a very quick double slur, (hammer and pull-off), so that the main note is reached a fraction of a second later. *Españoleta* is in the key of D minor, (relative minor of F major), and it is wise to learn this scale before embarking on the piece. The left-hand fingering in the second octave of the scale should be studied carefully, as much use is made of the second string.

New notes

Scale of D minor

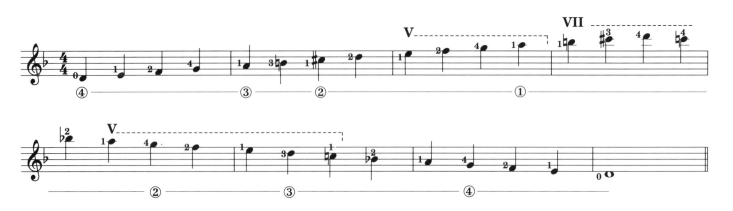

Matachin is the liveliest of the group, heavily ornamented, and like Paradetas lies for the most part in position two. In bar seventeen, the middle note of the chord (A), is played on the second string, fret ten. The G sharp in the next bar is also on string two but this time fret nine.

One last point relating to slurs. In bar eighteen of the Españoleta, and bars one, and five in Matachin, there are Mordents on the second string in chords where the *first* string is also being played. This means it is impossible to use the technique whereby the finger which is being pulled off comes to rest on the next string, as this will block the upper note of the chord. Instead we must make sure that the finger executing the slur clears this string, but that the slur still sounds clearly by a definite plucking movement of the finger, and not falling into the bad habit of simply lifting it off the string as this will produce a note which is scarcely audible.

Paradetas

Gaspar Sanz

Española

Gaspar Sanz

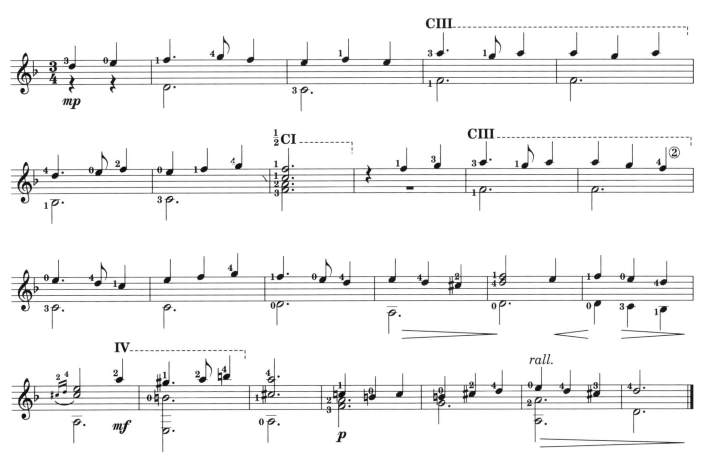

Matachin

Gaspar Sanz

45 SPANISH MUSIC IN THE SIXTEENTH CENTURY

The sixteenth century was the Golden Age for music in Spain. At the Royal Courts the instrument in vogue at that time was the vihuela, what perhaps might be termed the Spanish counterpart of the lute. Certainly the guitar existed in those times, but its more limited range and plebeian associations made it undesirable for serious performance and composition. In the same way as the lutenists used tablature, so the Spanish vihuelists employed a similar system. The first book of music for the vihuela appeared in 1535. It was by Luis Milan, and was entitled Libro de Musica de vihuela de mano Institulado El Maestro. Apparently, a whole school of vihuelists preceded Milan and his contemporaries, but because it was never published this music is not lost. Other famous volumes to emerge after Milan's, were by Narvaez (1538), Mudarra (1546), Valderrabano (1547), Pisador (1552)), Fuenllana (1554), Henestrosa (1557), Santa Maria (1563), and Daza (1567).

For this book, I have selected two short Sonetos from the Silva de Sirenas of 1547 by Enriquez de Valderrabano. Number VIII opens with some curious fingering, a full-barré for the first two beats. This is to allow the middle voice (A) to continue sounding, and also make it easier to get to the bass B. The barré comes off for the third beat, but then a half-barré comes into force in bar two. The third beat in this

bar can if you wish be fingered also with a half-barré, at fret three. The full-barré then comes back in bar three. Last note in bar six (C sharp), is fingered with fourth finger. This slightly awkward movement is to enable you to get to the next treble note smoothly. Notice how bars 13 and 14 are indicated with dynamics. This is to create an echo effect. Bar twenty should be studied separately, for what appears to be rather clumsy fingering turns out with a little practice to be fairly straight-forward. Soneta IX has fewer technical problems, but I would suggest that the first bar of the second half should be worked on, as it is easy to make this sound disjointed. Both pieces must be played with great attention to the voices or lines and clarity is of utmost importance. Try to make your performance of this music have a smoothness or LEGATO as it is termed, so there is a feeling of the notes moving onward in a horizontal line, rather than vertically.

We have a new fingering for the note D, which in certain places is not to be played as an open string, but instead fingered on string 5, fret 5, for example as in the opening chord.

At the end of Soneto IX there is what is called a first and second-time bar. The first time through the second half, play the First ending, and for the repeat play ending number Two.

Soneto No.8

E. de Valderrabano

Soneto No.9

E. de Valderrabano

Now, having learnt a number of pieces is the time to consider how to cut off unwanted bass notes, which if left ringing will affect and interfere with the harmonies of the piece.

I chose to introduce this technique towards the end of the book, simply because in my own experiences in teaching it has been too complicated a thing to teach early on, when people are still struggling with basic technique and learning notes.

There are at least four forms of damping, three in the right hand, and one in the left. The right-hand ones are the most commonly used and the methods are as follows:

In the case of the next string up having to be damped, e. g.,

simply play the second note as a rest-stroke with the thumb. This automatically cuts out the upper note.

With a lower bass string which must be stopped from sounding, e.g.,

the back of the thumb (preferably not the nail) is used to damp the lower string a fraction of a second before the next note is struck, (figure 40). This is hard, and should be practised just on open bass strings to begin with. Once learnt, it can be used in chordal passages such as the last two chords in the Larghetto by Sor, learnt several chapters ago. For the last two A's to sound clearly, the bass E must be cut in the manner described above.

Fig. 40

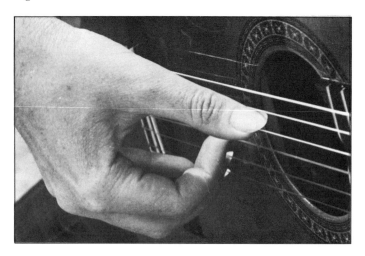

The third method is where the two strings are separated by another string, e.g.,

Here, after the second note has been struck, the thumb rests gently and for only a fraction of a second on the first note, so dampening it.

Left-hand damping is done simply by dabbing the tip of a finger onto an unwanted string. This technique is seldom used in classical guitar performance, and the student is best advised to concentrate and perfect the other methods described earlier. The backs (pads) of left-hand fingers are sometimes used for damping, whilst actually pressing down another string, e.g. 3rd finger on D (second string), can be used to dampen the open E (1st) string, but again this should not be attempted just yet.

When you have become familiar with these damping techniques, it will be necessary to go through your earlier pieces to check which bass notes should be stopped. This is not as bad as it seems, for in a little while you will find yourself doing it automatically.

To help you understand what needs to be done, I have set out the opening of What if a Day with explicit instructions on which bass notes to cut, and the technique for each. In chordal passages such as this, the rest stroke form of damping may be hard to control; due to the contrary action of the fingers. If so, simply place the thumb on the higher of the bass strings, after the lower one has been struck.

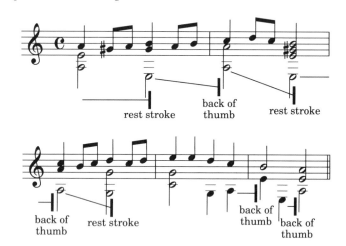

Fantasia — Francesco da Milano

The earliest compositions for lute in Italy can be found as far back as the very beginning of the 16th Century. An artistic peak was reached by the mid fifteen hundreds, with a general decline after about 1600, when the lute was rapidly being overtaken by keyboard instruments. As you will see from this beautiful example of a Fantasia by Francesco da Milano, the style of composition reflects very much the vocal style from the 15th Century and before, with its clarity of voicing, and the marvellous interwoven phrases using a great amount of imitation. The Fantasia was an extremely popular style of composition, but it should be remembered by the student that a piece of this nature must have a feeling of improvisation in the interpretation, and one must not be misled by the appearance of the music on paper. I would suggest the student does not take too much notice of the bar lines, but tries to convey the feeling of longer phrases in the music, the scale passages being pushed on in tempo slightly, with a free style of interpretation, whilst the cadences and more vertical harmonic sections be treated more strictly, so giving a steadying effect. Technically there should be nothing alarming to the student here, the notes falling under the fingers quite easily. However I would suggest a possible alternative fingering for bars 1 and 2 in order that the bass A can then be held for its full duration.

Fantasia

Francesco da Milano

47 SOME HINTS ON MEMORIZATION

A constantly recurring subject which students in classes or workshops are asking about, is memorization, or how to go about learning new pieces.

It is true that everybody has a different capacity for learning, but attention to this often neglected aspect of performance is I believe essential, not perhaps so much for the feeling of accomplishment at being able to perform a solo in public without the printed copy, but that by tackling a piece properly, one can explore the musical content in far greater depth, so enriching the performance. Too often I'm afraid we hear the expression "so-and-so played his pieces without music the other evening." I would draw your attention to the words without music. In many cases, a performance from memory can be like a boring string of notes, with either no thought to the phrasing or structure of the piece, or simply that the player is not quite ready to give a performance without the dots, and all his concentration is given to trying to play to the end without losing his way, very much a case of head down, gritting of the teeth, and hoping for the best. This obviously is no way to make music.

The composer is the same as the artist, indeed his task is perhaps a more difficult one. An artist's picture is a finished product, and a permanent impression of that artist's view of a scene, building, person, or whatever. We, the viewing public, can either accept that painting at a glance, calling it nice, pleasant, even beautiful, or we can study it in more depth, understanding how the artist has created a certain feeling, sense of depth, sense of movement, and so on. An artist whose paintings look rather like photographs, is very often more difficult or even impossible to study than somebody who transmits more of his own feelings technique, and is capable of imitating in his pictures anything he sees around him, but it is how to breathe life, energy, motion, warmth, sadness, into his work which separates the great from the not-so-great. People like Turner, Monet, Leonardo da Vinci, could with an inspired stroke or two of brush, pen, or pencil, give any of the above-mentioned feelings and much more to even the minutest detail in their work.

What has all this to do with playing the guitar? Everything. In most cases the composer cannot perform the piece for us, we have to interpret the vague series of dots on a page left to us by the composer. We must have the technique to be able to actually play those notes, but then must try to understand what the mood, feeling, character, of the piece is – what the composer is trying to say. We then go one step further than the painting, because every performer performs a given piece differently, tempos will vary, and any one performer will take a piece at a fractionally different tempo each time. We must learn and understand the language of the individual composer, what period he is from, the life he led, the circumstances in which the piece was written, and so on.

The actual process of learning a piece is something I have studied and researched for many years, asking fellow guitarists, pianists, violinists, etc., and have arrived at the following rough format.

Stage one is to read through the piece without the guitar in your hands. This way, we are not tied up with fingerings, barrés, and difficult technical problems which get in the way of the interpretation. Try to hear the piece in your mind. Study and note either mentally or actually on the page the shape and length of the phrases, where a top line is answered in a lower part, any slightly unusual harmonic progressions, etc. Also, any dynamic markings, and possible tonal contrasts you would like to use. Stage two is to play the piece through slowly, making use of it as sight-reading material. The technical problems will also make themselves apparent, and the tricky passages should be noted as well. Try to work out why a particular bar or passage causes you trouble, and see if you can devise a few short technical exercises based on that problem so that you do not get a fixation about that particular part of the piece and perhaps end up freezing at that point each time you play through the whole work. These exercises should always be started slowly, and only gradually increased in speed when you feel comfortable. It is not possible to play something fast if you cannot play it slowly, and this simple fact I'm afraid is overlooked by many.

Stage three is plotting milestones throughout the piece, that is links between one section and another where you can pause for breath as it were. Memory lapses do happen, even the best concert artists experience these almost every concert, and this is why these milestones are so valuable, for if you get absolutely stuck, one can then go on to the next one. Stage four is to practise the piece in sections, in the case of a long work such as the Chaconne of Bach perhaps only one or two pages might be tackled in a day. Thorough, concentrated practice is what we are aiming at, and six lines of a piece done well are better than six pages of aimless strumming. Stage five is to check whether you really know each section by either playing to a friend, or trying to write out the passage from memory. Also connected with this is the very important mental practice in which with time it can become possible to not only see the printed page in your mind, but also hear every minute detail of the score. What you are in fact doing is actually practising the piece, without the final stage of producing notes. When we read a new piece, it is a process of feeding in information from the page to the brain, where a conscious effort is made to store this accumulation of notes, fingerings, and sounds. It is after this that sleep plays an important part in memory, for it is whilst sleeping that all this information is sifted and stored in the subconscious ready to be called on in performance. The act of performing from memory is an out-going function, in which all the information flows out from the sub-conscious, allowing us to give an uninterrupted, and uncluttered performance. In fact the brain is working a split second ahead of the hands, for whilst one note is being played, the next note is already in the performer's mind. This is why the performer never really hears properly what he or she is doing, because the inner ear is already hearing the next note all the time. In mental practice, this also happens and it is just the actual sounding of the strings which is missing, everything else is happening, including the signals from the brain to the fingers. Many of the incidents of memory lapses are caused by the performer actually forgetting the sound of the piece, particularly so in modern music. It is not enough simply to rely upon finger patterns or movements. This is only one system. It is these things plus the sound of the piece, the shape of the phrase, the names of the notes, the structure of the harmony, the right hand fingering, even the feel of the left thumb on the guitar neck, which all go into the memory bank, and are recalled during performance.

Just to round off this chapter, stage six in the learning process would be to plan your practice on new pieces carefully. Never keep to the same piece for more than three or four days. Quite enough solid work will have been done in that time for the sub-conscious to take over, and the following three or four days should be devoted to another piece. It is beneficial to have a rest from a piece, and when you come back to it, you will be fresh and ready to go further ahead on it. The point is proved still further, by the hundreds of instances I have witnessed of players who have given up a piece because it has been too difficult, only to find six months or a year later that they now find it easier. In that time not only has their technique improved, but also the piece has had time to sink in mentally.

48 TWO-OCTAVE SCALE OF G MAJOR (ALTERNATIVE FINGERING)

Just before going on to learn the Catalan Folk Songs in the following chapter, we must tidy up one loose end by covering alternative fingering for the two-octave G Major scale.

In fact the left-hand fingering I have decided to introduce here may seem fussy in that it does not use any open string, but with practice this type of fingering is better, the fact that it is all on closed strings making it somehow easier to control. The whole scale is played at position two, and of course this fingering pattern can be used at any position from I to VII or even IX which means a whole range of scales becomes available with just one fingering.

Only one slightly unusual fingering occurs, and this is between the C on string three and the D on string two. The first finger may keep wanting to drop onto C sharp, which on close examination is a cover-up for a lazy third finger. With most people it is the third finger which is the weak member of the hand, due to the fact that it is closely linked to the middle finger. The older the person is who learns a musical instrument such as the guitar, the worse this problem can be. Children seldom have this trouble as the muscles and tendons are that much more supple and very quickly become accustomed to the demands of playing. However, even somebody who commences study at the tender age of say twenty-one will find it difficult, and may have to work very hard to catch up on lost time. To go back to our problem fingering, the first finger will often go onto C sharp as a panic move, the middle finger held by some mysterious force which in fact is the lazy third finger. It is probably a good idea when going up the scale to release the third finger when the C has been reached, at the same time positioning the middle finger over the D on the second string. This will achieve greater strength of the third finger due to this enforced lifting motion, coupled with the positioning of the middle finger over the second string.

Likewise, there is an alternative fingering for C major which can be used at various positions:

Scale of G major

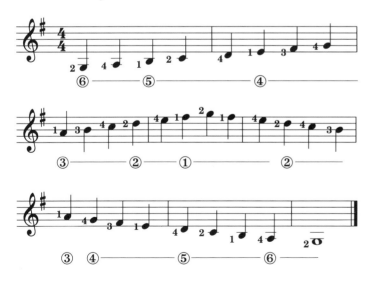

Study Opus 100, No.2 — Giuliani

This is a comparatively straightforward arpeggio study by Mauro Giuliani, the right hand pattern being exactly the same throughout. However, there are one or two left hand fingerings which are not so easy, although there is nothing incredibly difficult in the whole piece, all the notes being within the first five frets. Bars 1 – 3 are worthy of close study, as a full barré is used throughout and there is a tricky reversing of fingers 2 and 4 here. Also, the third finger has to go onto the bass A in bar 2, and then be removed again in bar 3, not as easy as it sounds bearing in mind all the other things going on at the same time. There are several places where guide fingers are used, e.g. bars 7 – 9. Here the 3rd finger should be kept down on D. The half barré in bars 37 and 38 should cover strings 3, 4 and 5.

Study Opus 100, No.2

M. Giuliani

49 CATALAN FOLK SONG

In this folksong El Rossinyol, I propose to go through in detail, describing how I would set about learning it, remembering what I discussed in the chapter on memorization. One thing which must be dealt with first however is the technique of producing harmonics. These are delicate bell-like notes which can either be played singly, in chords, (much favoured by composers such as the celebrated Brazilian Heitor Villa-Lobos), or as a melody on the upper strings with normal notes as an accompaniment on the lower strings. For now I shall deal with just the first of these. Two techniques are used for harmonics, and the resultant notes are called either **natural** or **artificial** harmonics depending on how they are executed. Natural harmonics are produced by simply resting the pad of a left-hand finger on the string without actually pressing it down. The right hand strikes the string, and at the same time, the left-hand finger is released so producing the harmonic, (figure 41). Natural harmonics can only really be played on certain frets, the strongest notes being at frets twelve and seven. They are also possible on several other frets, but generally only work well on top-class instruments. The left-hand finger should be positioned immediately over the fret, not behind it as we do when playing normal notes.

Fig. 41

The opening of El Rossinyol has a group of Natural Harmonics, which are repeated half way through the piece. Various composers have differing ways of indicating harmonics, and it has for some years been the subject of much confusion, but the method I use here seems to be used by the majority of people. The notes printed on the stave are an octave lower than the actual note produced by the harmonic. If we were to write them at actual pitch it would sometimes lead to confusion because of the leger lines.

Over the top of the notes appear the words Nat. Hars., self-explanatory I think, as indeed are Art. Hars., a little later on. The numbers which follow indicate the *frets* at which the harmonics are found, and of course the numbers below with the circles indicate the strings. Any left-hand finger may be used for natural harmonics, but where two different frets are used as in this piece, to avoid any rush, I would suggest fourth finger for the twelfth fret, and first finger for the

seventh. Here then are the opening notes for El Rossinyol. I find it best to use free-strokes for harmonics as a general rule.

Fig. 42

At the end of the piece there are some artificial harmonics. If you feel you have quite enough to think about for now, just play these last notes as normal notes at the pitch stated in the copy. For those brave ones who like a challenge, artificial harmonics are produced with a different technique, which to begin with at any rate, is difficult. The main point about them is that we can play them on any note and therefore are not restricted to certain frets. The idea is to read and finger the notes as if they were normal notes. So the first one E would be open first string. To produce an artificial harmonic, lightly rest the right-hand index finger twelve frets (one octave) higher than the note in question on the same string — in this case fret 12, first string. Now pluck the string with the third finger of the right hand using a free-stroke, (figure 42). As you pluck the string, release the index finger. With a little bit of practice you will be able to produce a good clear note. Now let us try the next one. This is D, second string, third fret. Once again the *right-hand* index finger rests lightly on that same string twelve frets higher than the note in question, (fret fifteen, string two). When plucked, the string will produce a high D. Remember, lift the right-hand index finger, not the left-hand finger. Once again the fret numbers are printed over the notes, but please do not forget that with artificial harmonics these apply to the right hand index finger.

Art. hars.

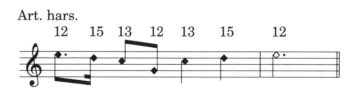

When you have practised the harmonics the remainder of the piece can be looked at. The folk songs of the province of Catalonia are quite different in style and character from the rest of Spain. Catalonia was only slightly influenced by Arabic orientalism, and the rugged coastline and mountains of this beautiful province inspired a wealth of superb romances and songs which contain great depth of feeling.

El Rossinyol is The Nightingale. It tells of a young girl and the message which she wishes the nightingale to take to her parents in France.

El Rossinyol

(trad. Catalan)
Arr. John Mills

Nightingale going to France
Tell my mother
Nightingale of the woodland
In your flight
Tell my mother
Nightingale
Do not tell so much to my father
Nightingale of the shady grove
In your flight
That a shepherd is my lover
Nightingale of the woodland
In your flight.

The opening harmonics are an introduction, and should be played slightly slower and more freely than the main tune which begins at the end of bar two. The tempo throughout the piece however should be very relaxed and easy. Guitar music does not often have *phrase marks* but I have included them in this piece to show how I would divide the piece up. Notice how the opening phrase is answered immediately on the bass. The fourth phrase is very short, and is more like an afterthought. This should be played a little more slowly. In bar four do not forget to cut the eighth-note

D and G in the bass line. Also the bass E in the following bar must be damped by placing the thumb back on after it has sounded the D. The fourth phrase is nice in that it ends not on the major harmony but in the relative minor. There is then a short link passage of arpeggio chords before the introduction appears once again (harmonics). In bar ten observe the natural sign cancelling out the key-signature of G major. From here on we are in the key of C major, this gradual shift of key being achieved by what is called a *modulation*. In bar twelve, watch out for the G's in the lower voice making sure you cut them by using firstly a rest stroke on the C (fourth note) with the index finger, and then a rest stroke with the thumb on the F which comes after the second G. The beginning of bar thirteen has an interesting technical point. The bass A must be stopped, but to do a rest stroke on the G is perhaps a little clumsy as there is a chord over the top. Here, it is perfectly acceptable to use the placement technique, that is touching the A string with the thumb after the next bass note has been played. Notice how the bass F in that same bar must be held for two beats. The way to do this is to use a pivot. Put the full barré down to begin with, then lift part of it to allow the open first and third strings to sound, keeping the bottom string depressed. The barré then goes back down for the C at the end of the bar.

50 MINUET BY J.S. BACH

One of the favourite composers of guitarists the world over is the great Johann Sebastian Bach. As an introduction to his music, I have included his celebrated Minuet in G Major, which appears in Bach's famous collection of pieces The Notebook of Anna Magdalena Bach. In the summer of 1720, Bach's first wife Maria Barbara died, an event which cast shadows on the composer's happy and fruitful period in Kothen. Eighteen months later, he married Anna Magdalena Wilcken, a singer at court since 1720. Later in 1725 Bach gave her a clavier exercise book containing two partitas in his own hand. The remainder of the book was then filled up by Anna Magdalena with a collection of shorter pieces, such as dances, arias, and chorals, most of them by Bach.

For the purposes of this book, the Minuet provides a not too difficult piece with clearly defined treble and bass lines. Unlike the last piece, every care must be taken to observe strictly the values of every note. An example will be found in bar two, where it is easy to let the D ring through the bar. Care must be taken to see that this does not creep into your performance. Music of the Baroque period is a vast subject and cannot really be discussed in this volume. It is not simply a matter of observing note values. There are very subtle rhythmical variations and accentuations which cannot be put down on the printed music. The composers of that time assumed every performer understood this language, and so we find very little prompting in the original manuscripts. Ornamentation, or 'embellishment' as it is sometimes called, was used virtually all the time, particularly on a repeated passage, with the addition of trills, mordents, etc. This not only added brilliance to the piece, but showed off the skills of the performer

as well. Ornamentation originally grew out of the need to support long notes which were difficult to sustain on the instruments of the period – it is a fascinating subject well worth study. However, please do not worry about this for the moment in learning the little Minuet in G. We are for the present really concerned with getting the correct notes as cleanly and as smoothly as possible. The very first pair of notes in the piece is something of a problem because we have to separate fingers 3 and 4. Make sure that neither finger collapses, and remember to keep the lower note sounding for two quarter notes. Don't forget that the F in bar seven is actually F sharp, (remember the key-signature). When going from bars 3 to 4, and from 11 to 12, notice how the bass B is fingered with the first finger. The second has just been used to depress the top F sharp, and obviously it would be foolish to make the finger leap back immediately for the B. Finally, there is a most interesting fingering in bar 13. The bass F sharp is fingered with third finger and the last note A with the fourth. This makes for a very easy progression into the next bar with the third finger having simply to slide up to the third fret for the bass G. The *A Tempo* at bar 9 means return to the original tempo.

In the second half of the piece, the high B (first note, bar 17), will be found at fret 7 on string 1. The left-hand fingering for the remainder of the bar requires a slight extension of the hand, stretching back down from the B to reach the G with 1st finger. However, this then enables the group of notes to be played comfortably on one string, and the use of the 2nd finger for the final note (G), brings you nicely into position for the next bar.

Minuet

J.S. Bach

Musette — Bach

This is a marvellous piece, very effective either in a group or on its own. There is much of great technical value to the student, slurs in the left hand, octave playing, and some excellent practise in thumb control for the right hand, with the thumb jumping across strings to negotiate the octaves in the bass line. One slightly unusual technique appears in bars 1, 2, 5, 6 and 12. Here, in the group of 16th notes, the last two have been slurred, and what I am suggesting is that the 3rd note of the group be played normally, and the last note be slurred by simply hammering down with the left hand without sounding the note with the right hand. To somebody who has not done this before, it may seem a somewhat strange way of doing it, but this technique works very well when practised. The guitar tuning is a little different for the Musette in that the 6th string is tuned to D, an octave below the open 4th string. A good way to tune is to play the harmonic at the 12th fret on the 6th string, and lower the pitch until the note thus produced is the same as the open 4th string. In this lowering of the 6th string, after a few minutes the pitch of the string will rise slightly. It is a good idea once the string has been lowered to twist it a couple of times holding the string between the right-hand thumb and index finger. This will help settle the string into the new tuning. However, it might be a help to also have the 6th string very slightly flat at the beginning of the piece, to compensate for any rise in pitch while the piece is being played.

67

Gavotte — Jelinek

I was introduced to the music of Ivan Jelinek by the fine Czechoslovakian guitarist Vladimir Mikulka, who has included some of his compositions in his recitals. Jelinek was born in 1683 and died in 1759, spending the whole of his life in the Benedictine Monastery of St. John below the Rock where he was organist. The Gavotte comes from a Suite in A Major for lute. How much Jelinek wrote for the instrument is not known, as only a handful of works remain. However, they are all fine compositions, showing a good understanding of the instrument, and an original creative intellect. Before learning this Gavotte, we should cover the scale of A Major, the key in which this piece is written. The fingering pattern I would suggest is one where the whole scale is played at position four, as this fingering can then be used for several other scales simply by beginning at different positions on the fingerboard (as with G major earlier).

The dynamic markings at the beginning indicate that the piece should be played forte the first time, and then piano on the repeat. There may seem to be an awful lot of half-barrés around in the piece, including two in bar 2. Here, the two barrés fall on different strings, the first across strings 2, 3, and 4, and the second across strings 3, 4, and 5. The dots which appear above or below several notes are staccato markings, these notes are to be halved in length with an appropriate rest to compensate. This has the effect of making the music 'spiky'.

Tarleton's Resurrection & Mrs Winter's Jump — Dowland

These are two of the best-known Dowland pieces, both appearing here in the key of A Major which was discussed in the notes on the Gavotte by Jelinek. Although the time signature says $\frac{6}{8}$ you should think of this first piece as being a steady two-in-the-bar, with a smooth unhurried flow. Please remember that the G's in bar 4 are to be played sharp. In bar 5 there appears a fairly big stretch combined with a full-barré. This has to be, because the 3rd finger is needed for the D sharp. A similar type of fingering problem occurs in the following bar also. At bar 7 we have a big jump up to position four, with the 4th finger pressing down top B. Here, in the jump, do try to position both 1st and 4th fingers whilst you are making this position change, as it is no use arriving at the new position and finding you have to scramble for the notes. Mrs. Winter's Jump is a more lively and light-hearted work, with a very attractive harmonic "twist" in bar 6, and a dotted rhythm in several bars which should be brought out clearly. Notice should be taken of the one and only barré in the piece which is a full barré commencing on the last chord of bar 10.

Tarleton's Resurrection

Mrs Winter's Jump

69

Study — Coste

Napeléon Coste was one of the most renowned guitar performers and composers in France during the 19th Century, although curiously he is rather neglected today by players and teachers. Born in 1806 near Doubs, it seems he was destined for a military career until a severe illness, which left him with a somewhat weakened constitution, ruled out any ideas in that direction. He had been learning the guitar from the age of six, and when at the age of eighteen the family moved to Valenciennes, Coste gave his first public performances which met with a considerable degree of sucess. When he was twenty-four, Coste moved to Paris to study with Fernando Sor. He lived after this in Faubourg St. Germain and was soon making a considerable name for himself as a performer and teacher. However, it was not until 1840 that he began to publish some of his compositions, and it was perhaps unforunate that he "arrived" a little late on the scene for the guitar was beginning to wane in popularity, and so his works never reached as wide a public as they deserved. His performing career was brought to an early halt when he fell during a concert and broke his right arm. His right arm never regained its suppleness, and Coste never again performed in public. He died in Paris in 1883. The short Study which appears here, is one of a fine collection of Studies Opus 38. There are many studies which should be used more widely I feel, although mostly they are only really for quite advanced students. This is not an easy piece, and requires some considerable dexterity particularly in the left hand, to ensure a smooth legato line. Bar 10 has an unusual fingering where the 3rd finger has to move round behind the 2nd. My advice here would be to have the 2nd finger just a little further away from the 3rd fret, so giving yourself more room to move the 3rd finger. Do not rush the 16th notes in bar 16, these are purely linking one phrase to the next, and a slight crescendo plus if anything a small amount of holding back in tempo gives a good result. Please notice the echo effect in bars 19 and 20, with the crescendo coming out of it—this is very important. From halfway through bar 26 to the end of the piece, I would be inclined to slow the tempo, as to maintain strict tempo here sounds if anything rather rushed. There are a lot of notes to get in, and it is better to let the piece relax at the end like this. One final point, in bar 17, the middle D of the first chord is to be found on string three, fret 7.

70

Study — Brian Sexton

Study — Brian Sexton

The first of the specially commissioned pieces for this tutor is by the Canadian guitarist and composer Brian Sexton, who is based in Newfoundland.

It has been my pleasure to make a number of tours in that beautiful country, and I am very happy to be able to present this short Study here.

At first glance, the format of the piece may appear confusing, but it really is quite straightforward. The opening section (eleven bars), is played twice, but the second time going straight onto the second ending $\boxed{2}$. The next section is then played up to the marking D.C. al Coda, at which point we begin the whole piece again, but this time at the end of bar 10 moving directly to the Coda.

There are several changes of time signature, but these are all fairly easy and should cause no problems. In moving from bars 1 to 2 an interesting problem for the left hand occurs, (also at the end of bar 3), for if we are to hold onto the middle A flat, the first finger should momentarily collapse onto a half-barré when the note F is played in the top part. This is not easy, but it is worth the time spent practising this particular technique, as pivots like this are being used more than ever these days.

In the passage commencing at bar 6, notice how the composer has intended the music to increase in speed and volume (accel. and cresc.) gradually through to bar 9, where it naturally becomes an Allegretto tempo.

During the second half of the piece be aware of how the indication for A Tempo and Ponticello commence in the three notes before the bar line, as this is the commencement of the new phrase.

There are a couple of new fingerings to check on here, in the second chord, the note A flat is to be found on string 3, fret 1. Also in bar 11, notice how the B in the second chord is not an open string, but taken on string 3 at fret 4.

Fantaisie — Julie Inglis

In this beautiful short Fantaisie by Julie Inglis much use is made of slightly "jazzy" harmonies, giving the piece a charm and warmth. A smooth legato line is called for to bring out the expressive character of this music, and the student should avoid any snatching of chords or passing notes.

We have a superb example in bar two where the full barré is only released when the A is struck. The last note (B flat) must follow smoothly, and in time. By the way, the two top notes of the very first chord of the piece are to be played at fret seven for the F sharp, and fret six for the C sharp. To arrive smoothly on the third chord, I would use a pivot or hinge barré on the previous chord. To execute a pivot means you have to press just the first string with the upper part of the index finger, the finger held straight as for a full barré, but angled up so that it is clear of the remaining strings (2–6). This will be clearly seen in Fig. 43.

At bar six the half barré should cover strings 3, 4, and 5, and in order to achieve a smooth legato line in the bass part I suggest sliding the first finger up from the B flat to the D natural, and the finger then collapsed on to the half barré. The A and D in bar eight are both to be found at fret 7 on their respective strings. Bar 14, do not forget that the last note is also a B flat. The barré in bars 15 and 16 covers the top five strings. Check carefully the left-hand fingering in bar 17 – the C sharp being played at fret six. The half barré in bar 19 covers strings 2, 3, and 4, while the one in bar 21 covers strings 3, 4, and 5. The bass note in bar 20 (F sharp) is found at fret 9, fifth string.

So a summary of notes where fingerings should be carefully checked would be as follows:

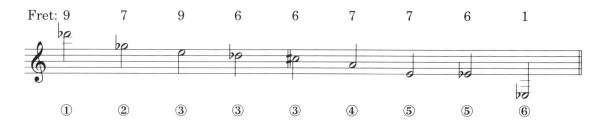

72

Fantaisie — Julie Inglis

Prelude — Lance Bosman

There are a number of problems confronting us in this next piece by Lance Bosman. Among these are constantly changing right-hand arpeggios, plus some left-hand fingering in fairly high positions which at first may prove a little troublesome.

The opening three bars are quite straightforward, requiring great accuracy however of the left-hand third finger. Bar 4 is where the first "problem" fingering appears, with the G sharp taken up on string four, fret six, and the D sharp on string three, fret eight. It is essential in bars like this to stick to a fixed right-hand pattern, otherwise it can easily become confusing—here, for example, the third string sounds higher than the second—if the right-hand fingering is not carefully practised, you will always stumble at this point.

In bar five, the C is played at fret ten, the high B at fret twelve, and the higher F sharp at fret eleven. Bar six, the last three notes are found at frets 6, 7, and 9 respectively, on the strings indicated.

The problem in bar seven is really the independence of the left hand finger during the last three notes. Note that the E should be held for two eighth-notes, and the 3rd finger pressing down A goes down after the E. I would here let the first note of the group (open G) continue sounding over the E. The first two notes of this bar are found at fret 8 on their respective strings. Do not forget to remove both 2nd and 3rd fingers before playing the first notes of bar 8.

In bar eleven, the half-barré at position six should ideally cover strings 2, 3, and 4. The last note here (F sharp) is played at fret seven on the second string, and the D sharp in bar twelve is at fret 8, 3rd string. The left-hand slurs in bars 13, 14, and 15 should present no real problems, apart from possibly those which do not begin on a strong beat. It is just a matter of getting used to the feel, as they should be played delicately. The final bar is a 2nd inversion of A Major with a major 7th (G sharp) and 9th (B). To allow every note to ring on, the G sharp and C sharp must be played at fret 6. The marking for the notes to continue sounding in this case to the end of the bar is as follows:

 This is very simple and clear, and saves cluttering up the remainder of the bar with notes and tie-lines.

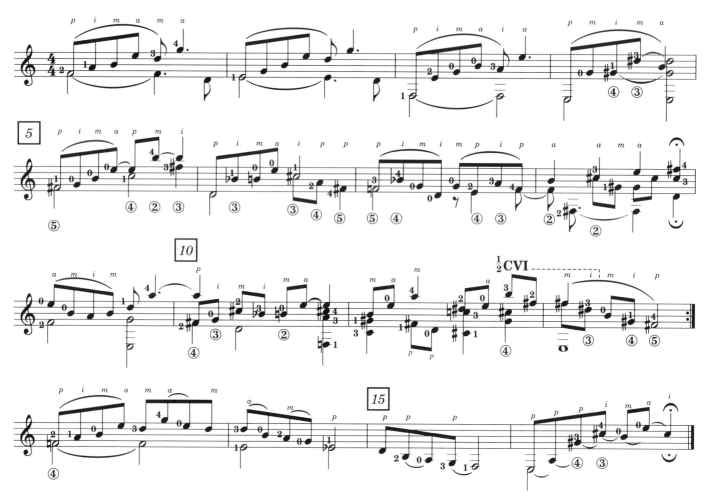

Canzona — Reginald Smith Brindle

The final piece in this tutor is the Canzona by Reginald Smith Brindle, who has been composing for the guitar since the mid 1940's, and is today one of the world's leading writers for the instrument.

The piece is, I believe, an appropriate way to close this book, for as well as being technically the most demanding of all the music included here, it will I hope open the student's eyes and ears to the many possibilities which lie tantalizingly ahead in the realms of the modern repertoire for the instrument.

At first it may be difficult to really comprehend the musical flow in the piece, in addition to which there are several bars with some technical difficulties, but the composer has a complete understanding of the fingerboard and you will find that gradually when your ear adjusts to the slightly unusual sounds the notes really do sit beneath the fingers beautifully! The markings such as those over the opening two chords indicate an up and down rasgueado with the index finger. Please follow very closely the dynamic indications, and try to build not only the volume, but also the quality and fullness of the tone as you approach the climax of a phrase. (There are two very good examples of this early on in bars 2 and 3, and bars 5 and 6.)

The passage between bars 20 and 24 is the most difficult part of the piece, as there are barrés everywhere, plus passage work in sixteenth-notes. All the barrés are full-barrés, and are not too demanding in themselves, but it is moving all the other fingers, combined with a couple of nasty leaps which make all this tricky. The answer as with all difficult problems is slow practice, taking each bar separately and concentrating on clarity, balance, and phrasing, not in any way making the notes staccato, particularly at the end of bars.

The passages marked "al 12°" are to be played with the right hand plucking an octave above the stopped note. However, in the case of a chord such as in the bar before the D.C. only the F sharp can really be played in this manner, so I would execute this chord by playing all three notes with the thumb at fret sixteen. In the final chord of the piece, a slightly angled thumb arpeggio is best, enabling us to play the top four notes of the chord approximately twelve frets higher. Start with the right-hand thumb plucking the bottom string about mid-way between frets 15 and 16, then angle the stroke so that you hit the top string immediately over fret 17.

The reason for plucking the strings in this way is to produce a tone quality which resembles the bassoon. The tone colour of an instrument is distinguished by quality of tone, which is determined by the partials or overtones. A note is not made up of a single sound at a given pitch. Just as white light can be broken up by the prism into many colours, so a single note played on an instrument is made up of a basic fundamental sound, above which are many very much softer notes, the pitch, strength, and number so determining the quality and colour of the sound. You can try this for yourself by plucking the low E string on your guitar, letting it sound for several seconds, and as the fundamental note dies, trying to hear the overtones. This is excellent training for the ear, and with practice will make you far more aware of the wonderful tonal possibilities of this beautiful instrument.

Some more new fingerings appear in the piece, so check carefully where you are playing the following notes;

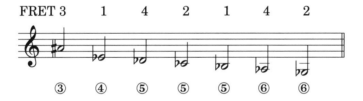

Canzona

Reginald Smith Brindle

9/00 (38121)